IF ONLY THEY COULD TALK

James Herriot grew up in Glasgow and qualified as a veterinary surgeon at Glasgow Veterinary College. Shortly afterwards, he took up a position as an assistant in a North Yorkshire practice where he remained, with the exception of his wartime service in the RAF, until his death in 1995.

JAMES HERRIOT

IF ONLY THEY COULD TALK

PAN BOOKS

First published 1970 by Michael Joseph Ltd

First published in paperback 1973 by Pan Books

This edition published 2006 by Pan Books
an imprint of Pan Macmillan Ltd
Pan Macmillan, 20 New Wharf Road, London N1 9RR
Basingstoke and Oxford
Associated companies throughout the world
www.panmacmillan.com

ISBN-13: 978-0-330-44708-9
ISBN-10: 0-330-44708-4

1 3 5 7 9 8 6 4 2

A CIP catalogue record for this book is available from
the British Library.

Printed and bound in Great Britain by
Mackays of Chatham plc, Chatham, Kent

To
EDDIE STRAITON
with gratitude and affection

CHAPTER ONE

They didn't say anything about this in the books, I thought, as the snow blew in through the gaping doorway and settled on my naked back.

I lay face down on the cobbled floor in a pool of nameless muck, my arm deep inside the straining cow, my feet scrabbling for a toe-hold between the stones. I was stripped to the waist and the snow mingled with the dirt and the dried blood on my body. I could see nothing outside the circle of flickering light thrown by the smoky oil lamp which the farmer held over me.

No, there wasn't a word in the books about searching for your ropes and instruments in the shadows; about trying to keep clean in a half bucket of tepid water; about the cobbles digging into your chest. Nor about the slow numbing of the arms, the creeping paralysis of the muscles as the fingers tried to work against the cow's powerful expulsive efforts.

There was no mention anywhere of the gradual exhaustion, the feeling of futility and the little far-off voice of panic.

My mind went back to that picture in the obstetrics book. A cow standing in the middle of a gleaming floor while a sleek veterinary surgeon in a spotless parturition overall inserted his arm to a polite distance. He was relaxed and smiling, the farmer and his helpers were smiling, even the cow was smiling. There was no dirt or blood or sweat anywhere.

That man in the picture had just finished an excellent lunch and had moved next door to do a bit of calving just for the sheer pleasure of it, as a kind of dessert. He hadn't crawled shivering from his bed at two o'clock in the morning and bumped over twelve miles of frozen snow, staring sleepily ahead till the lonely farm showed in the headlights. He hadn't climbed half a mile of white fell-side to the doorless barn where his patient lay.

I tried to wriggle my way an extra inch inside the cow. The calf's head was back and I was painfully pushing a thin, looped rope towards its lower jaw with my finger tips. All the time my arm was being squeezed between the calf and the bony pelvis. With every straining effort from the cow the pressure became almost unbearable, then she would relax and I would push the rope another inch. I wondered how long I would be able to keep this up. If I didn't snare that jaw soon I would never get the calf away. I groaned, set my teeth and reached forward again.

Another little flurry of snow blew in and I could almost hear the flakes sizzling on my sweating back. There was sweat on my forehead too, and it trickled into my eyes as I pushed.

There is always a time at a bad calving when you begin to wonder if you will ever win the battle. I had reached this stage.

Little speeches began to flit through my brain. 'Perhaps it would be better to slaughter this cow. Her pelvis is so small and narrow that I can't see a calf coming through,' or 'She's a good fat animal and really of the beef type, so don't you think it would pay you better to get the butcher?' or perhaps 'This is a very bad presentation. In a roomy cow it would be simple enough to bring the head round but in this case it is just about impossible.'

Of course, I could have delivered the calf by embryotomy – by passing a wire over the neck and sawing off the head. So many of these occasions ended with the floor strewn with heads, legs, heaps of intestines. There were thick text books devoted to the countless ways you could cut up a calf.

But none of it was any good here, because this calf was alive. At my furthest stretch I had got my finger as far as the commissure of the mouth and had been startled by a twitch of the little creature's tongue. It was unexpected because calves in this position are usually dead, asphyxiated by the acute flexion of the neck and the pressure of the dam's powerful contractions. But this one had a spark of life in it and if it came out it would have to be in one piece.

I went over to my bucket of water, cold now and bloody, and silently soaped my arms. Then I lay down again, feeling the cobbles harder than ever against my chest. I worked my toes between the stones, shook the sweat from my eyes and for the hundredth time thrust an arm that felt like spaghetti into the cow; alongside the little dry legs of the calf, like sandpaper tearing against my flesh, then to the bend in the neck and so to the ear and then, agonizingly, along the side of the face towards the lower jaw which had become my major goal in life.

It was incredible that I had been doing this for nearly two hours; fighting as my strength ebbed to push a little noose round that jaw. I had tried everything else – repelling a leg, gentle traction with a blunt hook in the eye socket, but I was back to the noose.

It had been a miserable session all through. The farmer, Mr Dinsdale, was a long, sad, silent man of few words who always seemed to be expecting the worst to happen. He had a long, sad, silent son with him and the two of them had watched my efforts with deepening gloom.

But worst of all had been Uncle. When I had first entered the hillside barn I had been surprised to see a little bright-eyed old man in a pork pie hat settling down comfortably on a bale of straw. He was filling his pipe and clearly looking forward to the entertainment.

'Now then, young man,' he cried in the nasal twang of the West Riding. 'I'm Mr Dinsdale's brother. I farm over in Listondale.'

I put down my equipment and nodded. 'How do you do? My name is Herriot.'

The old man looked me over, piercingly. 'My vet is Mr Broomfield. Expect you'll have heard of him – everybody knows him, I reckon. Wonderful man, Mr Broomfield, especially at calving. Do you know, I've never seen 'im beat yet.'

I managed a wan smile. Any other time I would have been delighted to hear how good my colleague was, but somehow not now, not now. In fact, the words set a mournful little bell tolling inside me.

'No, I'm afraid I don't know Mr Broomfield,' I said, taking off my jacket and, more reluctantly, peeling my shirt over my head. 'But I haven't been around these parts very long.'

Uncle was aghast. 'You don't know him! Well you're the only one as doesn't. They think the world of him in Listondale, I can tell you.' He lapsed into a shocked silence and applied a match to his pipe. Then he shot a glance at my goose-pimpled torso. 'Strips like a boxer does Mr Broomfield. Never seen such muscles on a man.'

A wave of weakness coursed sluggishly over me. I felt suddenly leaden-footed and inadequate. As I began to lay out my ropes and instruments on a clean towel the old man spoke again.

'And how long have you been qualified, may I ask?'

'Oh, about seven months.'

'Seven months!' Uncle smiled indulgently, tamped down his tobacco and blew out a cloud of rank, blue smoke. 'Well, there's nowt like a bit of experience, I always says. Mr Broomfield's been doing my work now for over ten years and he really knows what he's about. No, you can 'ave your book learning. Give me experience every time.'

I tipped some antiseptic into the bucket and lathered my arms carefully. I knelt behind the cow.

'Mr Broomfield always puts some special lubricating oils on his arms first,' Uncle said, pulling contentedly on his pipe. 'He says you get infection of the womb if you just use soap and water.'

I made my first exploration. It was the burdened moment all vets go through when they first put their hand into a cow. Within seconds I would know whether I would be putting on my jacket in fifteen minutes or whether I had hours of hard labour ahead of me.

I was going to be unlucky this time; it was a nasty presentation. Head back and no room at all; more like being inside an undeveloped heifer than a second calver. And she was bone dry – the 'waters' must have come away from her hours ago. She had been running out on the high fields and had started to calve a week before her time; that was why they had had to bring her into this half-ruined barn. Anyway, it would be a long time before I saw my bed again.

'Well now, what have you found, young man?' Uncle's penetrating voice cut through the silence. 'Head back, eh? You won't have much trouble, then. I've seen Mr Broomfield do 'em like that – he turns calf right round and brings it out back legs first.'

I had heard this sort of nonsense before. A short time in practice had taught me that all farmers were experts with other farmers' live stock. When their own animals were in trouble they tended to rush to the phone for the vet, but with their neighbours' they were confident, knowledgeable and full of helpful advice. And another phenomenon I had observed was that their advice was usually regarded as more valuable than the vet's. Like now, for instance; Uncle was obviously an accepted sage and the Dinsdales listened with deference to everything he said.

'Another way with a job like this,' continued Uncle, 'is to get a few strong chaps with ropes and pull the thing out, head back and all.'

I gasped as I felt my way around. 'I'm afraid it's impossible to turn a calf completely round in this small space. And to pull it out without bringing the head round would certainly break the mother's pelvis.'

The Dinsdales narrowed their eyes. Clearly they thought I was hedging in the face of Uncle's superior knowledge.

And now, two hours later, defeat was just round the corner. I was just about whacked. I had rolled and grovelled on the filthy cobbles while the Dinsdales watched me in morose silence and Uncle kept up a non-stop stream of comment. Uncle, his ruddy face glowing with delight, his little eyes sparkling, hadn't had such a happy night for years. His long trek up the hillside had been repaid a hundredfold. His vitality was undiminished; he had enjoyed every minute.

As I lay there, eyes closed, face stiff with dirt, mouth hanging open, Uncle took his pipe in his hand and leaned forward on his straw bale. 'You're about beat, young man,' he said with deep satisfaction. 'Well, I've never seen Mr Broomfield beat but he's had a lot of experience. And what's more, he's strong, really strong. That's one man you couldn't tire.'

Rage flooded through me like a draught of strong spirit. The right thing to do, of course, would be to get up, tip the bucket of bloody water over Uncle's head, run down the hill and drive away; away from Yorkshire, from Uncle, from the Dinsdales, from this cow.

Instead, I clenched my teeth, braced my legs and pushed with everything I had; and with a sensation of disbelief I felt my noose slide over the sharp little incisor teeth and into the calf's mouth. Gingerly, muttering a prayer, I pulled on the thin rope with my left hand and felt the slipknot tighten. I had hold of that lower jaw.

At last I could start doing something. 'Now hold this rope, Mr Dinsdale, and just keep a gentle tension on it. I'm going to repel the calf and if you pull steadily at the same time, the head ought to come round.'

'What if the rope comes off?' asked Uncle hopefully.

I didn't answer. I put my hand in against the calf's shoulder and began to push against the cow's contractions. I felt the small body moving away from me. 'Now a steady pull, Mr Dinsdale, without jerking.' And to myself, 'Oh God, don't let it slip off.'

The head was coming round. I could feel the neck straightening against my arm, then the ear touched my elbow. I let go the shoulder and grabbed the little muzzle. Keeping the teeth away from the vaginal wall with my hand, I guided the head till it was resting where it should be, on the fore limbs.

Quickly I extended the noose till it reached behind the ears. 'Now pull on the head as she strains.'

'Nay, you should pull on the legs now,' cried Uncle.

'Pull on the bloody head rope, I tell you!' I bellowed at the top of my voice and felt immediately better as Uncle retired, offended, to his bale.

With traction the head was brought out and the rest of the body followed easily. The little animal lay motionless on the cobbles, eyes glassy and unseeing, tongue blue and grossly swollen.

'It'll be dead. Bound to be,' grunted Uncle, returning to the attack.

I cleared the mucus from the mouth, blew hard down the throat and began artificial respiration. After a few pressures on the ribs, the calf gave a gasp and the eyelids flickered. Then it started to inhale and one leg jerked.

Uncle took off his hat and scratched his head in disbelief. 'By gaw, it's alive. I'd have thowt it'd sure to be dead after you'd messed about all that time.' A lot of the fire had gone out of him and his pipe hung down empty from his lips.

'I know what this little fellow wants,' I said. I grasped the calf by its fore legs and pulled it up to its mother's head. The cow was stretched out on her side, her head extended wearily along the rough floor. Her ribs heaved, her eyes were almost closed; she looked past caring about anything. Then she felt the calf's body against her face and there was a transformation; her eyes opened wide and her muzzle began a snuffling exploration of the new object. Her interest grew with every sniff and she struggled on to her chest, nosing and probing all over the calf, rumbling deep in her chest. Then she began to lick him methodically. Nature provides the perfect stimulant massage for a time like this and the little creature arched his back as the coarse papillae on the tongue dragged along his skin. Within a minute he was shaking his head and trying to sit up.

I grinned. This was the bit I liked. The little miracle. I felt it was something that would never grow stale no matter how often I saw it. I cleaned as much of the dried blood and filth from my body as I could, but most of it had caked on my skin and not even my finger nails would move it. It would have to wait for the hot bath at home. Pulling my shirt over my head, I felt as though I had been beaten for a long time with a thick stick. Every muscle ached. My mouth was dried out, my lips almost sticking together.

A long, sad figure hovered near. 'How about a drink?' asked Mr Dinsdale.

I could feel my grimy face cracking into an incredulous smile. A vision of hot tea well laced with whisky swam before me. 'That's very kind of you, Mr Dinsdale, I'd love a drink. It's been a hard two hours.'

'Nay,' said Mr Dinsdale looking at me steadily, 'I meant for the cow.'

I began to babble. 'Oh yes, of course, certainly, by all means give her a drink. She must be very thirsty. It'll do her good. Certainly, certainly, give her a drink.'

I gathered up my tackle and stumbled out of the barn. On the moor it was still dark and a bitter wind whipped over the snow, stinging my eyes. As I plodded down the slope, Uncle's voice, strident and undefeated, reached me for the last time.

'Mr Broomfield doesn't believe in giving a drink after calving. Says it chills the stomach.'

CHAPTER TWO

It was hot in the rickety little bus and I was on the wrong side where the July sun beat on the windows. I shifted uncomfortably inside my best suit and eased a finger inside the constricting white collar. It was a foolish outfit for this weather but a few miles ahead, my prospective employer was waiting for me and I had to make a good impression.

There was a lot hanging on this interview; being a newly

qualified veterinary surgeon in this year of 1937 was like taking out a ticket for the dole queue. Agriculture was depressed by a decade of government neglect, the draught horse which had been the mainstay of the profession was fast disappearing. It was easy to be a prophet of doom when the young men emerging from the colleges after a hard five years' slog were faced by a world indifferent to their enthusiasm and bursting knowledge. There were usually two or three situations vacant in the 'Record' each week and an average of eighty applicants for each one.

It hadn't seemed true when the letter came from Darrowby in the Yorkshire Dales. Mr Siegfried Farnon MRCVS would like to see me on the Friday afternoon; I was to come to tea and if we were mutually suited I could stay on as assistant. I had grabbed at the lifeline unbelievingly; so many friends who had qualified with me were unemployed or working in shops or as labourers in the shipyards that I had given up hope of any other future for myself.

The driver crashed his gears again as he went into another steep bend. We had been climbing steadily now for the last fifteen miles or so, moving closer to the distant blue swell of the Pennines. I had never been in Yorkshire before but the name had always raised a picture of a county as stodgy and unromantic as its pudding; I was prepared for solid worth, dullness and a total lack of charm. But as the bus groaned its way higher I began to wonder. The formless heights were resolving into high, grassy hills and wide valleys. In the valley bottoms, rivers twisted among the trees and solid grey-stone farmhouses lay among islands of cultivated land which pushed bright green promontories up the hillsides into the dark tide of heather which lapped from the summits.

I had seen the fences and hedges give way to dry stone walls which bordered the roads, enclosed the fields and climbed endlessly over the surrounding fells. The walls were everywhere, countless miles of them, tracing their patterns high on the green uplands.

But as I neared my destination the horror stories kept forcing their way into my mind; the tales brought back to college by veterans hardened and embittered by a few months of practice. Assistants were just little bits of dirt to be starved and worked into the ground by the principals who were heartless and vicious to a man. Dave Stevens, lighting a cigarette with trembling hand: 'Never a night off or a half day. He made me wash the car, dig the garden, mow the lawn, do the family shopping. But when he told me to sweep the chimney I left.' Or Willie Johnstone: 'First job I had to do was pass the stomach tube on a horse. Got it into the trachea instead of the oesophagus. Couple of quick pumps and down went the horse with a hell of a crash – dead as a hammer. That's when I started these grey hairs.' Or that dreadful one they passed around about Fred Pringle. Fred had trocharized a bloated cow and the farmer had been so impressed by the pent up gas hissing from the abdomen that Fred had got carried away and applied his cigarette lighter to the canula. A roaring sheet of flame had swept on to some straw bales and burned the byre to the ground. Fred had taken up a colonial appointment immediately afterwards – Leeward Islands wasn't it?

Oh hell, that one couldn't be true. I cursed my fevered imagination and tried to shut out the crackling of the inferno, the terrified bellowing of the cattle as they were led to safety. No, it couldn't be as bad as that; I rubbed my sweating palms on my knees and tried to concentrate on the man I was going to meet.

Siegfried Farnon. Strange name for a vet in the Yorkshire Dales. Probably a German who had done his training in this country and decided to set up in practice. And it wouldn't have been Farnon in the beginning; probably Farrenen. Yes, Siegfried Farrenen. He was beginning to take shape; short, fat, roly poly type with merry eyes and a bubbling laugh. But at the same time I had trouble with the obtruding image of a hulking, cold-eyed, bristle-skulled Teuton more in keeping with the popular idea of the practice boss.

I realized the bus was clattering along a narrow street which opened on to a square where we stopped. Above the window of an unpretentious grocer shop I read 'Darrowby Co-operative Society'. We had arrived.

I got out and stood beside my battered suitcase, looking about me. There was something unusual and I couldn't put my finger on it at first. Then I realized what it was – the silence. The other passengers had dispersed, the driver had switched off his engine and there was not a sound or a movement anywhere. The only visible sign of life was a group of old men sitting round the clock tower in the centre of the square but they might have been carved from stone.

Darrowby didn't get much space in the guide books but when it was mentioned it was described as a grey little town' on the river Darrow with a cobbled market place and little of interest except its two ancient bridges. But when you looked at it, its setting was beautiful on the pebbly river where the houses clustered thickly and straggled unevenly along the lower slopes of Herne Fell. Everywhere in Darrowby, in the streets, through the windows of the houses you could see the Fell rearing its calm, green bulk more than two thousand feet above the huddled roofs.

There was a clarity in the air, a sense of space and airiness that made me feel I had shed something on the plain, twenty miles behind. The confinement of the city, the grime, the smoke – already they seemed to be falling away from me.

Trengate was a quiet street leading off the square and I had my first sight of Skeldale House. I knew it was the right place before I was near enough to read 'S. Farnon MRCVS' on the old fashioned brass plate hanging slightly askew on the iron railings. I knew by the ivy which climbed untidily over the mellow brick to the topmost windows. It was what the letter had said – the only house with ivy; and this could be where I would work for the first time as a veterinary surgeon.

Now that I was here, right on the doorstep, I felt breathless, as though I had been running. If I got the job, this was where

I would find out about myself. There were many things to prove.

But I liked the look of the old house. It was Georgian with a fine, white-painted doorway. The windows, too, were white – wide and graceful on the ground floor and first storey but small and square where they peeped out from under the overhanging tiles far above. The paint was flaking and the mortar looked crumbly between the bricks, but there was a changeless elegance about the place. There was no front garden and only the railings separated the house from the street a few feet away.

I rang the doorbell and instantly the afternoon peace was shattered by a distant baying like a wolf pack in full cry. The upper half of the door was of glass and, as I peered through, a river of dogs poured round the corner of a long passage and dashed itself with frenzied yells against the door. If I hadn't been used to animals I would have turned and run for my life. As it was I stepped back warily and watched the dogs as they appeared, sometimes two at a time, at the top of their leap, eyes glaring, jaws slavering. After a minute or two of this I was able to sort them out and I realized that my first rough count of about fourteen was exaggerated. There were, in fact, five; a huge fawn greyhound who appeared most often as he hadn't so far to jump as the others, a cocker spaniel, a Scottie, a whippet and a tiny, short-legged hunt terrier. This terrier was seldom seen since the glass was rather high for him, but when he did make it he managed to get an even more frantic note into his bark before he disappeared.

I was thinking of ringing the bell again when I saw a large woman in the passage. She rapped out a single word and the noise stopped as if by magic. When she opened the door the ravening pack was slinking round her feet ingratiatingly, showing the whites of their eyes and wagging their tucked-in tails. I had never seen such a servile crew.

'Good afternoon,' I said with my best smile. 'My name is Herriot.'

The woman looked bigger than ever with the door open. She was about sixty but her hair, tightly pulled back from her forehead, was jet black and hardly streaked with grey. She nodded and looked at me with grim benevolence, but she seemed to be waiting for further information. Evidently, the name struck no answering spark.

'Mr Farnon is expecting me. He wrote asking me to come today.'

'Mr Herriot?' she said thoughtfully. 'Surgery is from six to seven o'clock. If you wanted to bring a dog in, that would be your best time.'

'No, no,' I said, hanging on to my smile. 'I'm applying for the position of assistant. Mr Farnon said to come in time for tea.'

'Assistant? Well, now, that's nice.' The lines in her face softened a little. 'I'm Mrs Hall. I keep house for Mr Farnon. He's a bachelor, you know. He never said anything to me about you, but never mind, come in and have a cup of tea. He shouldn't be long before he's back.'

I followed her between whitewashed walls, my feet clattering on the tiles. We turned right at the end into another passage and I was beginning to wonder just how far back the house extended when I was shown into a sunlit room.

It had been built in the grand manner, high-ceilinged and airy with a massive fireplace flanked by arched alcoves. One end was taken up by a french window which gave on a long, high-walled garden. I could see unkempt lawns, a rockery and many fruit trees. A great bank of peonies blazed in the hot sunshine and at the far end, rooks cawed in the branches of a group of tall elms. Above and beyond were the green hills with their climbing walls.

Ordinary looking furniture stood around on a very worn carpet. Hunting prints hung on the walls and books were scattered everywhere, some on shelves in the alcoves but others piled on the floor in the corners. A pewter pint pot occupied a prominent place at one end of the mantelpiece. It was an interesting pot. Cheques and bank notes had been stuffed into it till they bulged out of the top and overflowed on to the hearth beneath. I was studying this with astonishment when Mrs Hall came in with a tea tray.

'I suppose Mr Farnon is out on a case.' I said.

'No, he's gone through to Brawton to visit his mother. I can't really say when he'll be back.' She left me with my tea.

The dogs arranged themselves peacefully around the room and, except for a brief dispute between the Scottie and the cocker spaniel about the occupancy of a deep chair, there was no sign of their previous violent behaviour. They lay regarding me with friendly boredom and, at the same time, fighting a losing battle against sleep. Soon the last nodding head had fallen back and a chorus of heavy breathing filled the room.

But I was unable to relax with them. A feeling of let-down gripped me; I had screwed myself up for an interview and I was left dangling. This was all very odd. Why should anyone write for an assistant, arrange a time to meet him and then go to visit his mother? Another thing – if I was engaged, I would be living in this house, yet the housekeeper had no instructions to prepare a room for me. In fact, she had never even heard of me.

My musings were interrupted by the door bell ringing and the dogs, as if touched by a live wire, leaped screaming into the air and launched themselves in a solid mass through the door. I wished they didn't take their duties so seriously. There was no sign of Mrs Hall so I went out to the front door where the dogs were putting everything into their fierce act.

'Shut up!' I shouted and the din switched itself off. The five dogs cringed abjectly round my ankles, almost walking on their knees. The big greyhound got the best effect by drawing his lips back from his teeth in an apologetic grin.

I opened the door and looked into a round, eager face. Its owner, a plump man in wellington boots leaned confidently against the railings.

'Hello, 'ello, Mr Farnon in?'

'Not at the moment. Can I help you?'

'Aye, give 'im a message when he comes in. Tell 'im Bert Sharpe of Barrow Hills has a cow wot wants borin' out?'

'Boring out?'

'That's right, she's nobbut going on three cylinders.'

'Three cylinders?'

'Aye and if we don't do summat she'll go wrang in 'er ewer, won't she?'

'Very probably.'

'Don't want felon, do we?'

'Certainly not.'

'OK, you'll tell 'im, then. Ta-ta.'

I returned thoughtfully to the sitting-room. It was disconcerting but I had listened to my first case history without understanding a word of it.

I had hardly sat down when the bell rang again. This time I unleashed a frightening yell which froze the dogs when they were still in mid air; they took the point and returned, abashed, to their chairs.

This time it was a solemn gentleman with a straightly adjusted cloth cap resting on his ears, a muffler knotted precisely over his adam's apple and a clay pipe growing from the exact centre of his mouth. He removed the pipe and spoke with a rich, unexpected accent.

'Me name's Mulligan and I want Misther Farnon to make up some midicine for me dog.'

'Oh, what's the trouble with your dog, Mr Mulligan?'

He raised a questioning eyebrow and put a hand to his ear. I tried again with a full blooded shout.

'What's the trouble?'

He looked at me doubtfully for a moment. 'He's womitin', sorr. Womitin' bad.'

I immediately felt on secure ground now and my brain began to seethe with diagnostic procedures. 'How long after eating does he vomit?'

The hand went to the ear again. 'Phwhat's that?'

21

I leaned close to the side of his head, inflated my lungs and bawled: 'When does he womit – I mean vomit?'

Comprehension spread slowly across Mr Mulligan's face. He gave a gentle smile. 'Oh aye, he's womitin'. Womitin' bad, sorr.'

I didn't feel up to another effort so I told him I would see to it and asked him to call later. He must have been able to lip-read me because he seemed satisfied and walked away.

Back in the sitting-room, I sank into a chair and poured a cup of tea. I had taken one sip when the bell rang again. This time, a wild glare from me was enough to make the dogs cower back in their chairs; I was relieved they had caught on so quickly.

Outside the front door a lovely, red-haired girl was standing. She smiled, showing a lot of very white teeth.

'Good afternoon,' she said in a loud, well-bred voice. 'I am Diana Brompton. Mr Farnon is expecting me for tea.'

I gulped and clung to the door handle. 'He's asked YOU to tea?'

The smile became fixed. 'Yes, that is correct,' she said, spelling the words out carefully, 'He asked me to tea.'

'I'm afraid Mr Farnon isn't at home. I can't say when he'll be back.'

The smile was plucked away. 'Oh,' she said, and she got a lot into the word. 'At any rate, perhaps I could come in.'

'Oh, certainly, do come in. I'm sorry.' I babbled, suddenly conscious that I had been staring, open mouthed at her.

I held open the door and she brushed past me without a word. She knew her way about because, when I got to the first corner, she had disappeared into the room. I tiptoed past the door and broke into a gallop which took me along another thirty yards or so of twisting passage to a huge, stone-flagged kitchen. Mrs Hall was pottering about there and I rushed at her.

'There's a young lady here, a Miss Brompton. She's come to tea, too.' I had to fight an impulse to pluck at her sleeve.

Mrs Hall's face was expressionless. I thought she might have started to wave her arms about, but she didn't even seem surprised.

'You go through and talk to her and I'll bring a few more cakes,' she said.

'But what the heck am I going to talk to her about? How long is Mr Farnon going to be?'

'Oh, just chat to her for a bit. I shouldn't think he'll be very long,' she said calmly.

Slowly, I made my way back to the sitting-room and when I opened the door the girl turned quickly with the makings of another big smile. She made no attempt to hide her disgust when she saw it was only me.

'Mrs Hall thinks he should be back fairly soon. Perhaps you would join me in a cup of tea while you're waiting.'

She gave me a quick glance which raked me from my rumpled hair to my scuffed old shoes. I realized suddenly how grimy and sweaty I was after the long journey. Then she shrugged her shoulders and turned away. The dogs regarded her apathetically. A heavy silence blanketed the room.

I poured a cup of tea and held it out to her. She ignored me and lit a cigarette. This was going to be tough, but I could only try.

I cleared my throat and spoke lightly. 'I've only just arrived myself. I hope to be the new assistant.'

This time she didn't trouble to look round. She just said 'Oh' and again the monosyllable carried a tremendous punch.

'Lovely part of the world, this.' I said, returning to the attack.

'Yes.'

'I've never been in Yorkshire before, but I like what I've seen.'

'Oh.'

'Have you known Mr Farnon very long?'

'Yes.'

'I believe he's quite young – about thirty?'

23

'Yes.'

'Wonderful weather.'

'Yes.'

I kept at it with courage and tenacity for about five minutes, hunting for something original or witty, but finally, Miss Brompton, instead of answering, took the cigarette from her mouth, turned towards me and gave me a long, blank stare. I knew that was the end and shrank into silence.

After that, she sat staring out of the french window, pulling deeply at her cigarette, narrowing her eyes as the smoke trickled from her lips. As far as she was concerned, I just wasn't there.

I was able to observe her at will and she was interesting. I had never met a living piece of a society magazine before. Cool, linen dress, expensive-looking cardigan, elegant legs and the glorious red hair falling on her shoulders.

And yet here was a fascinating thought. She was sitting there positively hungering for a little fat German vet. This Farnon must have something.

The tableau was finally broken up when Miss Brompton jumped to her feet. She hurled her cigarette savagely into the fireplace and marched from the room.

Wearily, I got out of my chair. My head began to ache as I shuffled through the french window into the garden. I flopped down among the knee deep grass on the lawn and rested my back against a towering acacia tree. Where the devil was Farnon? Was he really expecting me or had somebody played a horrible practical joke on me? I felt suddenly cold. I had spent my last few pounds getting here and if there was some mistake I was in trouble.

But, looking around me, I began to feel better. The sunshine beat back from the high old walls, bees droned among the bright masses of flowers. A gentle breeze stirred the withered blooms of a magnificent wistaria which almost covered the back of the house. There was peace here.

I leaned my head against the bark and closed my eyes. I

could see Herr Farrenen, looking just as I had imagined him, standing over me. He wore a shocked expression.

'Wass is dis you haff done?' he spluttered, his fat jowls quivering with rage. 'You kom to my house under false pretences, you insult Fraulein Brompton, you trink my tea, you eat my food. Vat else you do, hein? Maybe you steal my spoons. You talk about assistant but I vant no assistant. Is best I telephone the police.'

Herr Farrenen seized the phone in a pudgy hand. Even in my dream, I wondered how the man could use such a completely corny accent. I heard the thick voice saying 'Hello, hello.'

And I opened my eyes. Somebody was saying 'Hello', but it wasn't Herr Farrenen. A tall, thin man was leaning against the wall, his hands in his pockets. Something seemed to be amusing him. As I struggled to my feet, he heaved himself away from the wall and held out his hand. 'Sorry you've had to wait. I'm Siegfried Farnon.'

He was just about the most English looking man I had ever seen. Long, humorous, strong-jawed face. Small, clipped moustache, untidy, sandy hair. He was wearing an old tweed jacket and shapeless flannel trousers. The collar of his check shirt was frayed and the tie carelessly knotted. He looked as though he didn't spend much time in front of a mirror.

Studying him, I began to feel better despite the ache in my neck where it had rested against the tree. I shook my head to get my eyes fully open and tufts of grass fell from my hair. 'There was a Miss Brompton here,' I blurted out. 'She came to tea. I explained you had been called away.'

Farnon looked thoughtful, but not put out. He rubbed his chin slowly. 'Mm, yes – well, never mind. But I do apologize for being out when you arrived. I have a shocking memory and I just forgot.'

It was the most English voice, too.

Farnon gave me a long, searching look, then he grinned. 'Let's go inside. I want to show you round the place.'

CHAPTER THREE

The long offshoot behind the house had been the servants' quarters in grander days. Here, everything was dark and narrow and poky as if in deliberate contrast with the front.

Farnon led me to the first of several doors which opened off a passage where the smell of ether and carbolic hung on the air. 'This,' he said, with a secret gleam in his eye as though he were about to unveil the mysteries of Aladdin's cave, 'is the dispensary.'

The dispensary was an important place in the days before penicillin and the sulphonamides. Rows of gleaming Winchester bottles lined the white walls from floor to ceiling. I savoured the familiar names: Sweet Spirits of Nitre, Tincture of Camphor, Chlorodyne, Formalin, Salammoniac, Hexamine, Sugar of Lead, Linimentum Album, Perchloride of Mercury, Red Blister. The lines of labels were comforting.

I was an initiate among old friends. I had painfully accumulated their lore, ferreting out their secrets over the years. I knew their origins, actions and uses, and their maddeningly varied dosage. The examiner's voice— 'And what is the dose for the horse? – and the cow? – and the sheep? – and the pig? – and the dog? – and the cat?'

These shelves held the vets' entire armoury against disease and, on a bench under the window, I could see the instruments for compounding them; the graduated vessels and beakers, the mortars and pestles. And underneath, in an open cupboard, the medicine bottles, piles of corks of all sizes, pill boxes, powder papers.

As we moved around, Farnon's manner became more and more animated. His eyes glittered and he talked rapidly. Often, he reached up and caressed a Winchester on its shelf; or he would lift out a horse ball or an electuary from its box, give it a friendly pat and replace it with tenderness.

'Look at this stuff, Herriot,' he shouted without warning. 'Adrevan! This is the remedy, par excellence, for red worms in horses. A bit expensive, mind you – ten bob a packet. And these gentian violet pessaries. If you shove one of these into a cow's uterus after a dirty cleansing, it turns the discharges a very pretty colour. Really looks as though it's doing something. And have you seen this trick?'

He placed a few crystals of resublimated iodine on a glass dish and added a drop of turpentine. Nothing happened for a second then a dense cloud of purple smoke rolled heavily to the ceiling. He gave a great bellow of laughter at my startled face.

'Like witchcraft, isn't it? I use it for wounds in horses' feet. The chemical reaction drives the iodine deep into the tissues.'

'It does?'

'Well, I don't know, but that's the theory, and anyway, you must admit it looks wonderful. Impresses the toughest client.'

Some of the bottles on the shelves fell short of the ethical standards I had learned in college. Like the one labelled 'Colic Drench' and featuring a floridly drawn picture of a horse rolling in agony. The animal's face was turned outwards and wore an expression of very human anguish. Another bore the legend 'Universal Cattle Medicine' in ornate script – 'A Sovereign Remedy for coughs, chills, scours, pneumonia, milk fever, gargett and all forms of indigestion.' At the bottom of the label, in flaring black capitals was the assurance, 'Never Fails to Give Relief'.

Farnon had something to say about most of the drugs. Each one had its place in his five years' experience of practice; they all had their fascination, their individual mystique. Many of the bottles were beautifully shaped, with heavy glass stoppers and their Latin names cut deeply into their sides; names familiar to physicians for centuries, gathering fables through the years.

The two of us stood gazing at the gleaming rows without any idea that it was nearly all useless and that the days of the old medicines were nearly over. Soon they would be hustled into oblivion by the headlong rush of the new discoveries and they would never return.

'This is where we keep the instruments.' Farnon showed me into another little room. The small animal equipment lay on green baize shelves, very neat and impressively clean. Hypodermic syringes, whelping forceps, tooth scalers, probes, searchers, and, in a place of prominence, an ophthalmoscope.

Farnon lifted it lovingly from its black box. 'My latest purchase,' he murmured, stroking its smooth shaft. 'Wonderful thing. Here, have a peep at my retina.'

I switched on the bulb and gazed with interest at the glistening, coloured tapestry in the depths of his eye. 'Very pretty. I could write you a certificate of soundness.'

He laughed and thumped my shoulder. 'Good, I'm glad to hear it. I always fancied I had a touch of cataract in that one.'

He began to show me the large animal instruments which hung from hooks on the walls. Docking and firing irons, bloodless castrators, emasculators, casting ropes and hobbles, calving ropes and hooks. A new, silvery embryotome hung in the place of honour, but many of the instruments, like the drugs, were museum pieces. Particularly the blood stick and fleam, a relic of medieval times, but still used to bring the rich blood spouting into a bucket.

'You still can't beat it for laminitis,' Farnon declared seriously.

We finished up in the operating room with its bare white walls, high table, oxygen and ether anaesthetic outfit and a small sterilizer.

'Not much small animal work in this district.' Farnon smoothed the table with his palm. 'But I'm trying to encourage it. It makes a pleasant change from lying on your belly in a cow house. The thing is, we've got to do the job right. The old castor oil and prussic acid doctrine is no good at all. You probably know that a lot of the old hands won't look at a dog or a cat, but the profession has got to change its ideas.'

He went over to a cupboard in the corner and opened the door. I could see glass shelves with a few scalpels, artery forceps, suture needles and bottles of catgut in spirit. He took out his handkerchief and flicked at an auroscope before closing the doors carefully.

'Well, what do you think of it all?' he asked as he went out into the passage.

'Great,' I replied. 'You've got just about everything you need here. I'm really impressed.'

He seemed to swell visibly. The thin cheeks flushed and he hummed softly to himself. Then he burst loudly into song in a shaky baritone, keeping time with our steps as we marched along.

Back in the sitting-room, I told him about Bert Sharpe. 'Something about boring out a cow which was going on three cylinders. He talked about her ewer and felon – I didn't quite get it.'

Farnon laughed. 'I think I can translate. He wants a Hudson's operation doing on a blocked teat. Ewer is the udder and felon the local term for mastitis.'

'Well, thanks. And there was a deaf Irishman, a Mr Mulligan . . .'

'Wait a minute.' Farnon held up a hand. 'Let me guess – womitin'?'

'Aye, womitin' bad, sorr.'

'Right, I'll put up another pint of bismuth carb for him. I'm in favour of long range treatment for this dog. He looks like an airedale but he's as big as a donkey and has a moody disposition. He's had Joe Mulligan on the floor a few times – just gets him down and worries him when he's got nothing better to do. But Joe loves him.'

'How about the womitin'?'

'Doesn't mean a thing. Natural reaction from eating every bit of rubbish he finds. Well, we'd better get out to Sharpe's.

And there are one or two other visits – how about coming with me and I'll show you a bit of the district.'

Outside the house, Farnon motioned me towards a battered Hillman and, as I moved round to the passenger's side, I shot a startled glance at the treadless tyres, the rusty bodywork, the almost opaque windscreen with its network of fine cracks. What I didn't notice was that the passenger seat was not fixed to the floor but stood freely on its sledge-like runners. I dropped into it and went over backwards, finishing with my head on the rear seat and my feet against the roof. Farnon helped me up, apologizing with great charm, and we set off.

Once clear of the market place, the road dipped quite suddenly and we could see all of the Dale stretching away from us in the evening sunshine. The outlines of the great hills were softened in the gentle light and a broken streak of silver showed where the Darrow wandered on the valley floor.

Farnon was an unorthodox driver. Apparently captivated by the scene, he drove slowly down the hill, elbows resting on the wheel, his chin cupped in his hands. At the bottom of the hill he came out of his reverie and spurted to seventy miles an hour. The old car rocked crazily along the narrow road and my movable seat slewed from side to side as I jammed my feet against the floor boards.

Then he slammed on the brakes, pointed out some pedigree Shorthorns in a field and jolted away again. He never looked at the road in front; all his attention was on the countryside around and behind him. It was that last bit that worried me, because he spent a lot of time driving fast and looking over his shoulder at the same time.

We left the road at last and made our way up a gated lane. My years of seeing practice had taught me to hop in and out very smartly as students were regarded primarily as gate-opening machines. Farnon, however, thanked me gravely every time and once I got over my surprise I found it refreshing.

We drew up in a farmyard. 'Lame horse here,' Farnon said.

A strapping Clydesdale gelding was brought out and we watched attentively as the farmer trotted him up and down.

'Which leg do you make it?' my colleague asked. 'Near fore? Yes, I think so, too. Like to examine it?'

I put my hand on the foot, feeling how much hotter it was than the other. I called for a hammer and tapped the wall of the hoof. The horse flinched, raised the foot and held it trembling for a few seconds before replacing it carefully on the ground. 'Looks like pus in the foot to me.'

'I'll bet you're right,' Farnon said. 'They call it gravel around here, by the way. What do you suggest we do about it?'

'Open up the sole and evacuate the pus.'

'Right.' He held out a hoof knife. 'I'll watch your technique.'

With the uncomfortable feeling that I was on trial, I took the knife, lifted the foot and tucked it between my knees. I knew what I had to do – find the dark mark on the sole where the infection had entered and follow it down till I reached the pus. I scraped away the caked dirt and found not one, but several marks. After more tapping to find the painful area I selected a likely spot and started to cut.

The horn seemed as hard as marble and only the thinnest little shaving came away with each twist of the knife. The horse, too, appeared to appreciate having his sore foot lifted off the ground and gratefully leaned his full weight on my back. He hadn't been so comfortable all day. I groaned and dug him in the ribs with my elbow and, though it made him change his position for a second, he was soon leaning on again.

The mark was growing fainter and, after a final gouge with the knife, it disappeared altogether. I swore quietly and started on another mark. With my back at breaking point and the sweat trickling into my eyes, I knew that if this one petered out, too, I would have to let the foot go and take a rest. And with Farnon's eye on me I didn't want to do that.

Agonizingly, I hacked away and, as the hole deepened, my knees began an uncontrollable trembling. The horse rested happily, his fifteen hundredweight cradled by this thoughtful human. I was wondering how it would look when I finally fell flat on my face when, under the knife blade, I saw a thin spurt of pus followed by a steady trickle.

'There it goes,' the farmer grunted. 'He'll get relief now.'

I enlarged the drainage hole and dropped the foot. It took me a long time to straighten up and when I stepped back, my shirt clung to my back.

'Well done, Herriot.' Farnon took the knife from me and slipped it into his pocket. 'It just isn't funny when the horn is as hard as that.'

He gave the horse a shot of tetanus antitoxin then turned to the farmer. 'I wonder if you'd hold up the foot for a second while I disinfect the cavity.' The stocky little man gripped the foot between his knees and looked down with interest as Farnon filled the hole with iodine crystals and added some turpentine. Then he disappeared behind a billowing purple curtain.

I watched, fascinated, as the thick pall mounted and spread. I could locate the little man only by the spluttering noises from somewhere in the middle.

As the smoke began to clear, a pair of round, startled eyes came into view. 'By Gaw, Mr Farnon, I wondered what the 'ell had happened for a minute,' the farmer said between coughs. He looked down again at the blackened hole in the hoof and spoke reverently: 'It's wonderful what science can do nowadays.'

We did two more visits, one to a calf with a cut leg which I stitched, dressed and bandaged, then to the cow with the blocked teat.

Mr Sharpe was waiting, still looking eager. He led us into the byre and Farnon gestured towards the cow. 'See what you can make of it.'

I squatted down and palpated the teat, feeling the mass of thickened tissue half way up. It would have to be broken down by a Hudson's instrument and I began to work the thin metal spiral up the teat. One second later, I was sitting gasping in the dung channel with the neat imprint of a cloven hoof on my shirt front, just over the solar plexus.

It was embarrassing, but there was nothing I could do but sit there fighting for breath, my mouth opening and shutting like a stranded fish.

Mr Sharpe held his hand over his mouth, his innate politeness at war with his natural amusement at seeing the vet come to grief. 'I'm sorry, young man, but I owt to 'ave told you that this is a very friendly cow. She allus likes to shake hands.' Then, overcome by his own wit, he rested his forehead on the cow's back and went into a long paroxysm of silent mirth.

I took my time to recover, then rose with dignity from the channel. With Mr Sharpe holding the nose and Farnon lifting up the tail, I managed to get the instrument past the fibrous mass and by a few downward tugs I cleared the obstruction; but, though the precautions cramped the cow's style a little, she still got in several telling blows on my arms and legs.

When it was over, the farmer grasped the teat and sent a long white jet frothing on the floor. 'Capital! She's going on four cylinders now!'

CHAPTER FOUR

'We'll go home a different way.' Farnon leaned over the driving wheel and wiped the cracked windscreen with his sleeve. 'Over the Brenkstone Pass and down Sildale. It's not much further and I'd like you to see it.'

We took a steep, winding road, climbing higher and still higher with the hillside falling away sheer to a dark ravine where a rocky stream rushed headlong to the gentler country below. On the top, we got out of the car. In the summer dusk, a wild panorama of tumbling fells and peaks rolled away and lost itself in the crimson and gold ribbons of the Western sky. To the East, a black mountain overhung us, menacing in its naked black bulk. Huge, square-cut boulders littered the lower slopes.

I whistled softly as I looked around. This was different from the friendly hill country I had seen on the approach to Darrowby.

Farnon turned towards me. 'Yes, one of the wildest spots in England. A fearsome place in winter. I've known this pass to be blocked for weeks on end.'.

I pulled the clean air deeply into my lungs. Nothing stirred in the vastness, but a curlew cried faintly and I could just hear the distant roar of the torrent a thousand feet below.

It was dark when we got into the car and started the long descent into Sildale. The valley was a shapeless blur but points of light showed where the lonely farms clung to the hillsides.

We came to a silent village and Farnon applied his brakes violently. I tobogganed effortlessly across the floor on my mobile seat and collided with the windscreen. My head made a ringing sound against the glass but Farnon didn't seem to notice. 'There's a grand little pub here. Let's go in and have a beer.'

The pub was something new to me. It was, simply, a large kitchen, square and stone-flagged. An enormous fireplace and an old black cooking range took up one end. A kettle stood on the hearth and a single large log hissed and crackled, filling the room with its resinous scent.

About a dozen men sat on the high-backed settles which lined the walls. In front of them, rows of pint mugs rested on oak tables which were fissured and twisted with age.

There was a silence as we went in. Then somebody said 'Now then, Mr Farnon,' not enthusiastically, but politely, and this brought some friendly grunts and nods from the company. They were mostly farmers or farm workers taking their pleasure without fuss or excitement. Most were burnt red by the sun and some of the younger ones were tieless, muscular necks and chests showing through the open shirt fronts. Soft murmurs and clicks rose from a peaceful domino game in the corner.

Farnon guided me to a seat, ordered two beers and turned to face me. 'Well, you can have this job if you want it. Four quid a week and full board. OK?'

The suddenness struck me silent. I was in. And four pounds a week! I remembered the pathetic entries in the *Record*. 'Veterinary surgeon, fully experienced, will work for keep.' The BVMA had had to put pressure on the editor to stop him printing these cries from the heart. It hadn't looked so good to see members of the profession offering their services free. Four pounds a week was affluence.

'Thank you,' I said, trying hard not to look triumphant. 'I accept.'

'Good.' Farnon took a hasty gulp at his beer. 'Let me tell you about the practice. I bought it a year ago from an old man of eighty. Still practising, mind you, a real tough old character. But he'd got past getting up in the middle of the night, which isn't surprising. And, of course, in lots of other ways he had let things slide – hanging on to all the old ideas. Some of those ancient instruments in the surgery were his. One way and another, there was hardly any practice left and I'm trying to work it up again now. There's very little profit in it so far, but if we stick in for a few years, I'm confident we'll have a good business. The farmers are pleased to see a younger man taking over and they welcome new treatments and operations. But I'm having to educate them out of the three and sixpenny consulting fee the old chap used to charge and it's been a hard slog. These Dalesmen are wonderful people and you'll like them, but they don't like parting with their brass unless you can prove they are getting something in return.'

He talked on enthusiastically of his plans for the future, the drinks kept coming and the atmosphere in the pub thawed steadily. The place filled up as the regulars from the village streamed in, the noise and heat increased and by near closing time I had got separated from my colleague and was in the

35

middle of a laughing group I seemed to have known for years.

But there was one odd character who swam repeatedly into my field of vision. An elderly little man with a soiled white panama perched above a smooth, brown, time-worn face like an old boot. He was dodging round the edge of the group, beckoning and winking.

I could see there was something on his mind, so I broke away and allowed myself to be led to a seat in the corner. The old man sat opposite me, rested his hands and chin on the handle of his walking stick and regarded me from under drooping eyelids.

'Now then, young man, ah've summat to tell thee. Ah've been among beasts all me life and I'm going to tell tha summat.'

My toes began to curl. I had been caught this way before. Early in my college career I had discovered that all the older inhabitants of the agricultural world seemed to have the idea that they had something priceless to impart. And it usually took a long time. I looked around me in alarm but I was trapped. The old man shuffled his chair closer and began to talk in a conspiratorial whisper. Gusts of beery breath hit my face from six inches range.

There was nothing new about the old man's tale – just the usual recital of miraculous cures he had wrought, infallible remedies known only to himself and many little sidetracks about how unscrupulous people had tried in vain to worm his secrets from him. He paused only to take expert pulls at his pint pot; his tiny frame seemed to be able to accommodate a surprising amount of beer.

But he was enjoying himself and I let him ramble on. In fact I encouraged him by expressing amazement and admiration at his feats.

The little man had never had such an audience. He was a retired smallholder and it had been years since anybody had shown him the appreciation he deserved. His face wore a lopsided leer and his swimmy eyes were alight with friendship. But suddenly he became serious and sat up straight.

'Now, afore ye go, young man, I'm going to tell thee summat nobody knows but me. Ah could've made a lot o' money out o' this. Folks 'ave been after me for years to tell 'em but I never 'ave.'

He lowered the level in his glass by several inches then narrowed his eyes to slits. 'It's the cure for mallenders and sallenders in 'osses.'

I started up in my chair as though the roof had begun to fall in. 'You can't mean it,' I gasped. 'Not mallenders and sallenders.'

The old man looked smug. 'Ah, but ah do mean it. All you have to do is rub on this salve of mine and the 'oss walks away sound. He's better by that!' His voice rose to a thin shout and he made a violent gesture with his arm which swept his nearly empty glass to the floor.

I gave a low, incredulous whistle and ordered another pint. 'And you're really going to tell me the name of this salve?' I whispered.

'I am, young man, but only on one condition. Tha must tell no one. Tha must keep it to thaself, then nobody'll know but thee and me.' He effortlessly tipped half of his fresh pint down his throat. 'Just thee and me, lad.'

'All right, I promise you. I'll not tell a soul. Now what is this wonderful stuff?'

The old man looked furtively round the crowded room. Then he took a deep breath, laid his hand on my shoulder and put his lips close to my ear. He hiccuped once, solemnly, and spoke in a hoarse whisper. 'Marshmallow ointment.'

I grasped his hand and wrung it silently. The old man, deeply moved, spilled most of his final half pint down his chin.

But Farnon was making signals from the door. It was time to go. We surged out with our new friends, making a little island of noise and light in the quiet village street. A tow-haired young fellow in shirt sleeves opened the car door with natural courtesy and, waving a final goodnight, I plunged in. This time, the seat went over quicker than usual and I hurtled backwards, coming to rest with my head among some Wellingtons and my knees tucked underneath my chin.

A row of surprised faces peered in at me through the back window, but soon, willing hands were helping me up and the trick seat was placed upright on its rockers again. I wondered how long it had been like that and if my employer had ever thought of having it fixed.

We roared off into the darkness and I looked back at the waving group. I could see the little man, his panama gleaming like new in the light from the doorway. He was holding his finger to his lips.

CHAPTER FIVE

The past five years had been leading up to one moment and it hadn't arrived yet. I had been in Darrowby for twenty-four hours now and I still hadn't been to a visit on my own.

Another day had passed in going around with Farnon. It was a funny thing, but, for a man who seemed careless, forgetful and a few other things, Farnon was frustratingly cautious about launching his new assistant.

We had been over into Lidderdale today and I had met more of the clients – friendly, polite farmers who received me pleasantly and wished me success. But working under Farnon's supervision was like being back at college with the professor's eye on me. I felt strongly that my professional career would not start until I, James Herriot, went out and attended a sick animal, unaided and unobserved.

However, the time couldn't be very far away now. Farnon had gone off to Brawton to see his mother again. A devoted son, I thought wonderingly. And he had said he would be back late, so the old lady must keep unusual hours. But never mind about that – what mattered was that I was in charge.

I sat in an armchair with a frayed loose cover and looked out through the french windows at the shadows thrown by the evening sun across the shaggy lawn. I had the feeling that I would be doing a lot of this.

I wondered idly what my first call would be. Probably an anticlimax after the years of waiting. Something like a coughing calf or a pig with constipation. And maybe that would be no bad thing – to start with something I could easily put right. I was in the middle of these comfortable musings when the telephone exploded out in the passage. The insistent clamour sounded abnormally loud in the empty house. I lifted the receiver.

'Is that Mr Farnon?' It was a deep voice with a harsh edge to it. Not a local accent; possibly a trace of the South West.

'No, I'm sorry, he's out. This is his assistant.'

'When will he be back?'

'Not till late, I'm afraid. Can I do anything for you?'

'I don't know whether you can do anything for me or not.' The voice took on a hectoring tone. 'I am Mr Soames, Lord Hulton's farm manager. I have a valuable hunting horse with colic. Do you know anything about colic?'

I felt my hackles rising. 'I am a veterinary surgeon, so I think I should know something about it.'

There was a long pause, and the voice barked again. 'Well, I reckon you'll have to do. In any case, I know the injection the horse wants. Bring some arecoline with you. Mr Farnon uses it. And for God's sake, don't be all night getting here. How long will you be?'

'I'm leaving now.'

'Right.'

I heard the receiver bang down onto its rest. My face felt hot as I walked away from the phone. So my first case wasn't going to be a formality. Colics were tricky things and I had an aggressive know-all called Soames thrown in for good measure.

On the eight mile journey to the case, I re-read from memory the great classic, Caulton Reeks' Common Colics of the Horse.

I had gone through it so often in my final year that I could recite stretches of it like poetry. The well-thumbed pages hovered in front of me, phantom-like, as I drove.

This would probably be a mild impaction or a bit of spasm. Might have had a change of food or too much rich grass. Yes, that would be it; most colics were like that. A quick shot of arecoline and maybe some chlorodyne to relieve the discomfort and all would be well. My mind went back to the cases I had met while seeing practice. The horse standing quietly except that it occasionally eased a hind leg or looked round at its side. There was nothing to it, really.

I was elaborating this happy picture when I arrived. I drove into a spotless, gravelled yard surrounded on three sides by substantial loose boxes. A man was standing there, a broad-shouldered, thick-set figure, very trim in check cap and jacket, well-cut breeches and shiny leggings.

The car drew up about thirty yards away and, as I got out, the man slowly and deliberately turned his back on me. I walked across the yard, taking my time, waiting for the other to turn round, but he stood motionless, hands in pockets, looking in the other direction.

I stopped a few feet away but still the man did not turn. After a long time, and when I had got tired of looking at the back, I spoke.

'Mr Soames?'

At first the man did not move, then he turned very slowly. He had a thick, red neck, a ruddy face and small, fiery eyes. He made no answer but looked me over carefully from head to foot, taking in the worn raincoat, my youth, my air of inexperience. When he had completed his examination he looked away again.

'Yes, I am Mr Soames.' He stressed the 'Mr' as though it meant a lot to him. 'I am a very great friend of Mr Farnon.'

'My name is Herriot.'

Soames didn't appear to have heard. 'Yes, a clever man is Mr Farnon. We are great friends.'

'I understand you have a horse with colic.' I wished my voice didn't sound so high and unsteady.

Soames' gaze was still directed somewhere into the sky. He whistled a little tune softly to himself before replying. 'In there,' he said, jerking his head in the direction of one of the boxes. 'One of his lordship's best hunters. In need of expert assistance, I think.' He put a bit of emphasis on the 'expert'.

I opened the door and went inside. And I stopped as though I had walked into a wall. It was a very large box, deeply bedded with peat moss. A bay horse was staggering round and round the perimeter where he had worn a deep path in the peat. He was lathered in sweat from nose to tail, his nostrils were dilated and his eyes stared blankly in front of him. His head rolled about at every step and, through his clenched teeth, gobbets of foam dripped to the floor. A rank steam rose from his body as though he had been galloping.

My mouth had gone dry. I found it difficult to speak and when I did, it was almost in a whisper. 'How long has he been like this?'

'Oh, he started with a bit of belly ache this morning. I've been giving him black draughts all day, or at least this fellow has. I wouldn't be surprised if he's made a bloody mess of it like he does everything.'

I saw that there was somebody standing in the shadows in the corner; a large, fat man with a head collar in his hand.

'Oh, I got the draughts down him, right enough, Mr Soames, but they haven't done 'im no good.' The big man looked scared.

'You call yourself a horseman,' Soames said, 'but I should have done the damn job myself. I reckon he'd have been better by now.'

'It would take more than a black draught to help him,' I said. 'This is no ordinary colic.'

'What the hell is it, then?'

'Well, I can't say till I've examined him, but severe, continuous pain like that could mean a torsion – a twisted bowel.'

'Twisted bowel, my foot! He's got a bit of belly ache, that's all. He hasn't passed anything all day and he wants something to shift him. Have you got the arecoline with you?'

'If this is a torsion, arecoline would be the worst thing you could give him. He's in agony now, but that would drive him mad. It acts by contracting the muscles of the intestines.'

'God dammit,' snarled Soames. 'Don't start giving me a bloody lecture. Are you going to start doing something for the horse or aren't you?'

I turned to the big man in the corner. 'Slip on that head collar and I'll examine him.'

With the collar on, the horse was brought to a halt. He stood there, trembling and groaning as I passed a hand between ribs and elbows, feeling for the pulse. It was as bad as it could be – a racing, thready beat. I everted an eyelid with my fingers; the mucous membrane was a dark, brick red. The thermometer showed a temperature of a hundred and three.

I looked across the box at Soames. 'Could I have a bucket of hot water, soap and a towel, please?'

'What the devil for? You've done nothing yet and you want to have a wash?'

'I want to make a rectal examination. Will you please bring me the water?'

'God help us, I've never seen anything like this.' Soames passed a hand wearily over his eyes then swung round on the big man. 'Well, come on, don't stand around there. Get him his water and we'll maybe get something done.'

When the water came, I soaped my arm and gently inserted it into the animal's rectum. I could feel plainly the displacement of the small intestine on the left side and a tense, tympanitic mass which should not have been there. As I touched it, the horse shuddered and groaned again.

As I washed and dried my arms, my heart pounded. What was I to do? What could I say?

Soames was stamping in and out of the box, muttering to himself as the pain maddened animal writhed and twisted. 'Hold the bloody thing,' he bellowed at the horseman who was gripping the head collar. 'What the bloody hell are you playing at?'

The big man said nothing. He was in no way to blame but he just stared back stolidly at Soames.

I took a deep breath. 'Everything points to the one thing. I'm convinced this horse has a torsion.'

'All right then, have it your own way. He's got a torsion. Only for God's sake do something, will you? Are we going to stand in here all night?'

'There's nothing anybody can do. There is no cure for this. The important thing is to put him out of his pain as quickly as possible.'

Soames screwed up his face. 'No cure? Put him out of his pain? What rubbish is this you're talking? Just what are you getting at?'

I took a hold on myself. 'I suggest you let me put him down immediately.'

'What do you mean?' Soames' mouth fell open.

'I mean that I should shoot him now, straight away. I have a humane killer in the car.'

Soames looked as if he was going to explode. 'Shoot him! Are you stark raving mad? Do you know how much that horse is worth?'

'It makes no difference what he's worth, Mr Soames. He has been going through hell all day and he's dying now. You should have called me out long ago. He might live a few hours more but the end would be the same. And he's in dreadful pain, continuous pain.'

Soames sunk his head in his hands. 'Oh God, why did this have to happen to me? His lordship is on holiday or I'd call him out to try to make you see some sense. I tell you, if your boss had been here he'd have given that horse an injection and put him right in half an hour. Look here, can't we wait till Mr Farnon gets back tonight and let him have a look at him?'

Something in me leaped gladly at the idea. Give a shot of morphine and get away out of it. Leave the responsibility to somebody else. It would be easy. I looked again at the horse. He had recommenced his blind circling of the box, stumbling round and round in a despairing attempt to leave his agony behind. As I watched, he raised his lolling head and gave a little whinny. It was a desolate, uncomprehending, frantic sound and it was enough for me.

I strode quickly out and got the killer from the car. 'Steady his head,' I said to the big man and placed the muzzle between the glazing eyes. There was a sharp crack and the horse's legs buckled. He thudded down on the peat and lay still.

I turned to Soames who was staring at the body in disbelief. 'Mr Farnon will come round in the morning and carry out a post mortem. I'd like Lord Hulton to have my diagnosis confirmed.'

I put on my jacket and went out to the car. As I started the engine, Soames opened the door and pushed his head in. He spoke quietly but his voice was furious. 'I'm going to inform his lordship about this night's work. And Mr Farnon too. I'll let him know what kind of an assistant he's landed himself with. And let me tell you this. You'll be proved wrong at that post mortem tomorrow and then I'm going to sue you.' He banged the door shut and walked away.

Back at the surgery, I decided to wait up for my boss and I sat there trying to rid myself of the feeling that I had blasted my career before it had got started. Yet, looking back, I knew I couldn't have done anything else. No matter how many times I went over the ground, the conclusion was always the same.

It was 1 AM before Farnon got back. His evening with his mother had stimulated him. His thin cheeks were flushed and he smelt pleasantly of gin. I was surprised to see that he was wearing evening dress and though the dinner jacket was of old-fashioned cut and hung in loose folds on his bony frame, he still managed to look like an ambassador.

He listened in silence as I told him about the horse. He was about to comment when the phone rang. 'A late one,' he whispered, then 'Oh, it's you, Mr Soames.' He nodded at me and settled down in his chair. He was a long time saying 'Yes' and 'No' and 'I see', then he sat up decisively and began to speak.

'Thank you for ringing, Mr Soames, and it seems as though Mr Herriot did the only possible thing in the circumstances. No, I cannot agree. It would have been cruel to leave him. One of our duties is to prevent suffering. Well, I'm sorry you feel like that, but I consider Mr Herriot to be a highly capable veterinary surgeon. If I had been there I have no doubt I'd have done the same thing. Goodnight, Mr Soames, I'll see you in the morning.'

I felt so much better that I almost launched into a speech of gratitude, but in the end, all I said was 'Thanks'.

Farnon reached up into the glass-fronted cupboard above the mantelpiece and pulled out a bottle of whisky. He carelessly slopped out half a tumblerful and pushed it at me. He gave himself a similar measure and fell back into the armchair.

He took a deep swallow, stared for a few seconds at the amber fluid in the glass then looked up with a smile. 'Well, you certainly got chucked in at the deep end tonight, my boy. Your first case! And it had to be Soames, too.'

'Do you know him very well?'

'Oh, I know all about him. A nasty piece of work and enough to put anybody off their stroke. Believe me, he's no friend of mine. In fact, rumour has it that he's a bit of a crook. They say he's been feathering his nest for a long time at his lordship's expense. He'll slip up one day, I expect.'

The neat whisky burned a fiery path down to my stomach but I felt I needed it. 'I wouldn't like too many sessions like tonight's, but I don't suppose veterinary practice is like that all the time.'

'Well, not quite,' Farnon replied, 'but you never know what's in store for you. It's a funny profession, ours, you know. It offers unparalleled opportunities for making a chump of yourself.'

'But I expect a lot depends on your ability.'

'To a certain extent. It helps to be good at the job, of course, but even if you're a positive genius humiliation and ridicule are lurking just round the corner. I once got an eminent horse specialist along here to do a rig operation and the horse stopped breathing halfway through. The sight of that man dancing frantically on his patient's ribs taught me a great truth – that I was going to look just as big a fool at fairly regular intervals throughout my career.'

I laughed. 'Then I might as well resign myself to it right at the beginning.'

'That's the idea. Animals are unpredictable things so our whole life is unpredictable. It's a long tale of little triumphs and disasters and you've got to really like it to stick it. Tonight it was Soames, but another night it'll be something else. One thing, you never get bored. Here, have some more whisky.'

I drank the whisky and then some more and we talked. It seemed no time at all before the dark bulk of the acacia tree began to emerge from the grey light beyond the french window, a blackbird tried a few tentative pipes and Farnon was regretfully shaking the last drops from the bottle into his glass.

He yawned, jerked the knot out of his black tie and looked at his watch. 'Well, five o'clock. Who would have thought it? But I'm glad we had a drink together – only right to celebrate your first case. It was a right one, wasn't it?'

CHAPTER SIX

Two and a half hours sleep was a meagre ration but I made a point of being up by seven thirty and downstairs, shaved and scrubbed, by eight.

But I breakfasted alone. Mrs Hall, impassively placing scrambled eggs before me, told me that my employer had left some time ago to do the PM on Lord Hulton's horse. I wondered if he had bothered to go to bed at all.

I was busy with the last of the toast when Farnon burst into the room. I was getting used to his entrances and hardly jumped at all as he wrenched at the door handle and almost leaped into the middle of the carpet. He looked rosy and in excellent spirits.

'Anything left in that coffee pot? I'll join you for a cup.' He crashed down on a protesting chair. 'Well, you've nothing to worry about. The PM showed a classical torsion. Several loops of bowel involved – black and tympanitic. I'm glad you put the poor beggar down straight away.'

'Did you see my friend Soames?'

'Oh, he was there, of course. He tried to get in a few digs about you but I quietened him. I just pointed out that he had delayed far too long in sending for us and that Lord Hulton wasn't going to be too pleased when he heard how his horse had suffered. I left him chewing over that.'

The news did a lot to lighten my outlook. I went over to the desk and got the day book. 'Here are this morning's calls. What would you like me to do?'

Farnon picked out a round of visits, scribbled the list on a scrap of paper and handed it over. 'Here you are,' he said, 'A few nice, trouble-free cases to get yourself worked in.'

I was turning to leave when he called me back. 'Oh, there's one other thing I'd like you to do. My young brother is hitching from Edinburgh today. He's at the Veterinary College there and the term finished yesterday. When he gets within striking distance he'll probably give us a ring. I wonder if you'd slip out and pick him up?'

'Certainly. Glad to.'

'His name is Tristan, by the way.'

'Tristan?'

'Yes. Oh, I should have told you. You must have wondered about my own queer name. It was my father. Great Wagnerian. It nearly ruled his life. It was music all the time – mainly Wagner.'

'I'm a bit partial myself.'

'Ah well, yes, but you didn't get it morning noon and night like we did. And then to be stuck with a name like Siegfried. Anyway, it could have been worse – Wotan, for instance.'

'Or Pogner.'

Farnon looked startled. 'By golly, you're right. I'd forgotten about old Pogner. I suppose I've a lot to be thankful for.'

It was late afternoon before the expected call came. The voice at the other end was uncannily familiar.

'This is Tristan Farnon.'

'Gosh, you sound just like your brother.'

A pleasant laugh answered me. 'Everybody says that – oh, that's very good of you. I'd be glad of a lift. I'm at the Holly Tree Café on the Great North Road.'

After the voice I had been expecting to find a younger edition of my employer but the small, boyish-faced figure sitting on a rucksack could hardly have been less like him. He got up, pushed back the dark hair from his forehead and held out his hand. The smile was charming.

'Had much walking to do?' I asked.

'Oh, a fair bit, but I needed the exercise. We had a roughish end of term party last night.' He opened the car door and threw the rucksack into the back. As I started the engine he settled himself in the passenger seat as though it were a luxurious armchair, pulled out a paper packet of Woodbines, lit one with tender concentration and gulped the smoke down blissfully. He produced the *Daily Mirror* from a side pocket and shook it open with a sigh of utter content. The smoke, which had been gone a long time, began to wisp from his nose and mouth.

I turned West off the great highway and the rumble of traffic faded rapidly behind us. I glanced round at Tristan. 'You'll have just finished exams?' I said.

'Yes, pathology and parasitology.'

I almost broke one of my steadfast rules by asking him if he had passed, but stopped myself in time. It is a chancy business. But in any case, there was no shortage of conversation. Tristan had something to say about most of the news items and now and then he read out an extract and discussed it with me. I felt a growing conviction that I was in the presence of a quicker and livelier mind than my own. It seemed no time at all before we pulled up outside Skeldale House.

Siegfried was out when we arrived and it was early evening when he returned. He came in through the french window, gave me a friendly greeting and threw himself into an armchair. He had begun to talk about one of his cases when Tristan walked in.

The atmosphere in the room changed as though somebody had clicked a switch. Siegfried's smile became sardonic and he gave his brother a long, appraising look. He grunted a 'hello', then reached up and began to run his finger along the titles of the books in the alcove. He seemed absorbed in this for a few minutes and I could feel the tension building up. Tristan's expression had changed remarkably; his face had gone completely deadpan but his eyes were wary.

Siegfried finally located the book he was looking for, took it down from the shelf and began to leaf through it unhurriedly. Then, without looking up, he said quietly: 'Well, how did the exams go?'

Tristan swallowed carefully and took a deep breath. 'Did all right in parasitology,' he replied in a flat monotone.

Siegfried didn't appear to have heard. He had found something interesting in his book and settled back to read. He took his time over it, then put the book back on the shelf. He began again the business of going along the titles; still with his back to his brother, he spoke again in the same soft voice.

'How about pathology?'

Tristan was on the edge of his chair now, as if ready to make a run for it. His eyes darted from his brother to the book shelves and back again. 'Didn't get it,' he said tonelessly.

There was no reaction from Siegfried. He kept up his patient search for his book, occasionally pulling a volume out, glancing at it and replacing it carefully. Then he gave up the hunt, lay back in the chair with his arms dangling almost to the floor and looked at Tristan. 'So you failed pathology,' he said conversationally.

I was surprised to hear myself babbling with an edge of hysteria in my voice. 'Well now that's pretty good you know. It puts him in the final year and he'll be able to sit path. at Christmas. He won't lose any time that way and, after all, it's a tough subject.'

Siegfried turned a cold eye on me. 'So you think it's pretty good, do you?' There was a pause and a long silence which was broken by a totally unexpected bellow as he rounded on his brother. 'Well, I don't! I think it is bloody awful! It's a damned disgrace, that's what it is. What the hell have you been doing all this term, anyway? Boozing, I should think, chasing women, spending my money, anything but working. And now you've got the bloody nerve to walk in here and tell me you've failed pathology. You're lazy, that's your trouble, isn't it? You're bloody bone idle!'

He was almost unrecognizable. His face was darkly flushed and his eyes glared. He yelled wildly again at his brother. 'But I've had enough this time. I'm sick of you. I'm not going to work my fingers to the bloody bone to keep you up there idling your time away. This is the end. You're sacked, do you hear me. Sacked once and for all. So get out of here – I don't want to see you around any more. Go on, get out!'

Tristan, who had preserved an air of injured dignity throughout, withdrew quietly.

Writhing with embarrassment, I looked at Siegfried. He was showing the strain of the interview. His complexion had gone blotchy; he muttered to himself and drummed his fingers on the arm of the chair.

I was aghast at having to witness this break-up and I was grateful when Siegfried sent me on a call and I was able to get out of the room.

It was nearly dark when I got back and I drove round to the back lane and into the yard at the foot of the garden. The creaking of the garage doors disturbed the rooks in the great elms which overhung the buildings. Far up in the darkness there was a faint fluttering, a muffled cawing then silence. As I stood listening, I became aware of a figure in the gloom, standing by the yard door, looking down the garden. As the face turned towards me I saw it was Tristan.

Again, I felt embarrassed. It was an unfortunate intrusion when the poor fellow had come up here to brood alone. 'Sorry about the way things turned out,' I said awkwardly.

The tip of the cigarette glowed brightly as Tristan took a long pull. 'No, no, that's all right. Could have been a lot worse, you know.'

'Worse? Well, it's bad enough, isn't it? What are you going to do?'

'Do? What do you mean?'

'Well, you've been kicked out, haven't you? Where are you going to sleep tonight?'

'I can see you don't understand,' Tristan said. He took his cigarette from his mouth and I saw the gleam of very white teeth as he smiled. 'You needn't worry. I'm sleeping here and I'll be down to breakfast in the morning.'

'But how about your brother?'

'Siegfried? Oh, he'll have forgotten all about it by then.'

'Are you sure?'

'Dead sure. He's always sacking me and he always forgets. Anyway, things turned out very well. The only tricky bit back there was getting him to swallow that bit about the parasitology.'

I stared at the shadowy form by my side. Again, there was a rustling as the rooks stirred in the tall trees then settled into silence.

'The parasitology?'

'Yes. If you think back, all I said was that I had done all right. I wasn't any more specific than that.'

'Then you mean . . .?'

Tristan laughed softly and thumped my shoulder.

'That's right, I didn't get parasitology. I failed in both. But don't worry, I'll pass them at Christmas.'

CHAPTER SEVEN

I huddled deeper in the blankets as the strident brreeng-brreeng, brreeng-brreeng of the telphone echoed through the old house.

It was three weeks since Tristan's arrival and life at Skeldale House had settled into a fairly regular pattern. Every day began much the same with the phone ringing between seven and eight o'clock after the farmers had had the first look at their stock.

There was only one phone in the house. It rested on a ledge in the tiled passage downstairs. Siegfried had impressed on me that I shouldn't get out of bed for these early calls. He had delegated the job to Tristan; the responsibility would be good for him. Siegfried had been emphatic about it.

I listened to the ringing. It went on and on – it seemed to get louder. There was neither sound nor movement from Tristan's room and I waited for the next move in the daily drama. It came, as always, with a door crashing back on its hinges, then

Siegfried rushed out on to the landing and bounded down the stairs three at a time.

A long silence followed and I could picture him shivering in the draughty passage, his bare feet freezing on the tiles as he listened to the farmer's leisurely account of the animal's symptoms. Then the ting of the phone in its rest and the mad pounding of feet on the stairs as Siegfried made a dash for his brother's room.

Next a wrenching sound as the door was flung open, then a yell of rage. I detected a note of triumph; it meant Tristan had been caught in bed – a definite victory for Siegfried and he didn't have many victories. Usually, Tristan exploited his quick-dressing technique and confronted his brother fully dressed. It gave him a psychological advantage to be knotting his tie when Siegfried was still in pyjamas.

But this morning Tristan had overplayed his hand; trying to snatch the extra few seconds he was caught between the sheets. I listened to the shouts. 'Why didn't you answer the bloody phone like I told you? Don't tell me you're deaf as well as idle! Come on, out of it, out, out!'

But I knew Tristan would make a quick come-back. When he was caught in bed he usually scored a few points by being halfway through his breakfast before his brother came in.

Later, I watched Siegfried's face as he entered the dining-room and saw Tristan munching his toast happily, his *Daily Mirror* balanced against the coffee pot. It was as if he had felt a sudden twinge of toothache.

It all made for a strained atmosphere and I was relieved when I was able to escape to collect my things for the morning round. Down the narrow passage with its familiar, exciting smell of ether and carbolic and out into the high-walled garden which led to the yard where the cars were kept.

It was the same every morning but, to me, there was always the feeling of surprise. When I stepped out into the sunshine and the scent of flowers it was as though I was doing it for the first time. The clear air held a breath of the nearby moorland; after being buried in a city for five years it was difficult to take it all in.

I never hurried over this part. There could be an urgent case waiting but I still took my time. Along the narrow part between the ivy-covered wall and the long offshoot of the house where the wistaria climbed, pushing its tendrils and its withered blooms into the very rooms. Then past the rockery where the garden widened to the lawn, unkempt and lost looking but lending coolness and softness to the weathered brick. Around its borders flowers blazed in untidy profusion, battling with a jungle of weeds.

And so to the rose garden, then an asparagus bed whose fleshy fingers had grown into tall fronds. Further on were strawberries and raspberries. Fruit trees were everywhere, their branches dangling low over the path. Peaches, pears, cherries and plums were trained against the South wall where they fought for a place with wild-growing rambler roses.

Bees were at work among the flowers and the song of blackbirds and thrushes competed with the cawing of the rooks high up in the elms.

Life was full for me. There were so many things to find out and a lot I had to prove to myself. The days were quick and challenging and they pressed on me with their very newness. But it all stopped here in the garden. Everything seemed to have stopped here a long time ago. I looked back before going through the door into the yard and it was like suddenly coming across a picture in an old book; the empty, wild garden and the tall, silent house beyond. I could never quite believe it was there and that I was a part of it.

And the feeling was heightened when I went into the yard. It was square and cobbled and the grass grew in thick tufts between the stones. Buildings took up two sides; the two garages, once coach houses, a stable and saddle room, a loose box and a pig sty. Against the free wall a rusty iron pump hung over a stone water trough.

Above the stable was a hay loft and over one of the garages

a dovecot. And there was old Boardman. He, too, seemed to have been left behind from grander days, hobbling round on his lame leg, doing nothing in particular.

He grunted good morning from his cubby hole where he kept a few tools and garden implements. Above his head his reminders of the war looked down; a row of coloured prints of Bruce Bairnsfather cartoons. He had stuck them up when he came home in 1918 and there they were still, dusty and curled at the edges but still speaking to him of Kaiser Bill and the shell holes and muddy trenches.

Boardman washed a car sometimes or did a little work in the garden, but he was content to earn a pound or two and get back to his yard. He spent a lot of time in the saddle room, just sitting. Sometimes he looked round the empty hooks where the harness used to hang and then he would make a rubbing movement with his fist against his palm.

He often talked to me of the great days. 'I can see t'owd doctor now, standing on top step waiting for his carriage to come round. Big, smart looking feller he was. Allus wore a top hat and frock coat, and I can remember him when I was a lad, standing there, pulling on 'is gloves and giving his hat a tilt while he waited.'

Boardman's features seemed to soften and a light came into his eyes as though he were talking more to himself than to me. 'The old house was different then. A housekeeper and six servants there were and everything just so. And a full time gardener. There weren't a blade of grass out of place in them days and the flowers all in rows and the trees pruned, tidy-like. And this yard – it were t'owd doctor's favourite spot. He'd come and look over t' door at me sitting here polishing the harness and pass time o' day, quiet like. He were a real gentleman but you couldn't cross 'im. A few specks o' dust anywhere down here and he'd go nearly mad.

'But the war finished it all. Everybody's rushing about now. They don't care about them things now. They've no time, no time at all.'

He would look round in disbelief at the overgrown cobbles, the peeling garage doors hanging crazily on their hinges. At the empty stable and the pump from which no water flowed.

He was always friendly with me in an absent way, but with Siegfried he seemed to step back into his former character, holding himself up smartly and saying 'Very good, sir,' and saluting repeatedly with one finger. It was as though he recognized something there – something of the strength and authority of t'owd doctor – and reached out eagerly towards the lost days.

'Morning, Boardman,' I said, as I opened the garage door. 'How are you today?'

'Oh, middlin' lad, just middlin'.' He limped across and watched me get the starting handle and begin the next part of the daily routine. The car allotted to me was a tiny Austin of an almost forgotten vintage and one of Boardman's voluntary duties was towing it off when it wouldn't start. But this morning, surprisingly, the engine coughed into life after six turns.

As I drove round the corner of the back lane, I had the feeling, as I did every morning, that this was where things really got started. The problems and pressures of my job were waiting for me out there and at the moment I seemed to have plenty.

I had arrived in the Dales, I felt, at a bad time. The farmers, after a generation of neglect, had seen the coming of a prophet, the wonderful new vet, Mr Farnon. He appeared like a comet, trailing his new ideas in his wake. He was able, energetic and charming and they received him as a maiden would a lover. And now, at the height of the honeymoon, I had to push my way into the act, and I just wasn't wanted.

I was beginning to get used to the questions. 'Where's Mr Farnon?' – 'Is he ill or something?' – 'I expected Mr Farnon.' It was a bit daunting to watch their faces fall when they saw me walking on to their farms. Usually they looked past me hopefully and some even went and peered into the car to see if the man they really wanted was hiding in there.

And it was uphill work examining an animal when its owner

was chafing in the background, wishing with all his heart that I was somebody else.

But I had to admit they were fair. I got no effusive welcomes and when I started to tell them what I thought about the case they listened with open scepticism, but I found that if I got my jacket off and really worked at the job they began to thaw a little. And they were hospitable. Even though they were disappointed at having me they asked me into their homes. 'Come in and have a bit o' dinner,' was a phrase I heard nearly every day. Sometimes I was glad to accept and I ate some memorable meals with them.

Often, too, they would slip half a dozen eggs or a pound of butter into the car as I was leaving. This hospitality was traditional in the Dales and I knew they would probably do the same for any visitor, but it showed the core of friendliness which lay under the often unsmiling surface of these people and it helped.

I was beginning to learn about the farmers and what I found I liked. They had a toughness and a philosophical attitude which was new to me. Misfortunes which would make the city dweller want to bang his head against a wall were shrugged off with 'Aye, well, these things happen.'

It looked like being another hot day and I wound down the car windows as far as they would go. I was on my way to do a tuberculin test; the national scheme was beginning to make its first impact in the Dales and the more progressive farmers were asking for survey tests.

And this was no ordinary herd. Mr Copfield's Galloway cattle were famous in their way. Siegfried had told me about them. 'The toughest lot in this practice. There's eighty-five of them and none has ever been tied up. In fact, they've scarcely been touched by hand. They live out on the fells, they calve and rear their calves outside. It isn't often anybody goes near them so they're practically wild animals.'

'What do you do when there's anything wrong with them?' I had asked.

'Well, you have to depend on Frank and George — they're the two Copfield sons. They've been reared with those cattle since they were babies — started tackling the little calves as soon as they could walk, then worked up to the big ones. They're about as tough as the Galloways.'

Copfield's place was one of the bleak ones. Looking across the sparse pastures to the bald heights with their spreading smudges of heather it was easy to see why the farmer had chosen a breed hardier than the local shorthorns. But this morning the grim outlines were softened by the sunshine and there was a desert peace in the endless greens and browns.

Frank and George were not as I expected. The durable men who helped me in my daily jobs tended to be dark and lean with stringy muscles but the Copfields were golden haired and smooth skinned. They were good looking young men about my own age and their massive necks and wide spread of shoulder made their heads look small. Neither of them was tall but they looked formidable with their shirt sleeves rolled high to reveal wrestlers' arms and their thick legs encased in cloth gaiters. Both wore clogs.

The cattle had been herded into the buildings and they just about filled all the available accommodation. There were about twenty-five in a long passage down the side of the fold yard; I could see the ragged line of heads above the rails, the steam rising from their bodies. Twenty more occupied an old stable and two lots of twenty milled about in large loose boxes.

I looked at the black, untamed animals and they looked back at me, their reddish eyes glinting through the rough fringe of hair which fell over their faces. They kept up a menacing, bad-tempered swishing with their tails.

It wasn't going to be easy to get an intradermal injection into every one of them. I turned to Frank.

'Can you catch these beggars?' I asked.

'We'll 'ave a bloody good try,' he replied calmly, throwing a halter over his shoulder. He and his brother lit cigarettes before climbing into the passage where the biggest beasts were packed. I followed them and soon found that the tales I had heard about the Galloways hadn't been exaggerated. If I approached them from the front they came at me with their great hairy heads and if I went behind them they kicked me as a matter of course.

But the brothers amazed me. One of them would drop a halter on a beast, get his fingers into its nose and then be carried away as the animal took off like a rocket. They were thrown about like dolls but they never let go; their fair heads bobbed about incongruously among the black backs; and the thing that fascinated me was that through all the contortions the cigarettes dangled undisturbed.

The heat increased till it was like an oven in the buildings and the animals, their bowels highly fluid with their grass diet, ejected greenish-brown muck like non-stop geysers.

The affair was conducted in the spirit of a game with encouragement shouted to the man in action: 'Thou 'as 'im, Frank.' 'Sniggle 'im, George.' In moments of stress the brothers cursed softly and without heat: 'Get off ma bloody foot, thou awd bitch.' They both stopped work and laughed with sincere appreciation when a cow slashed me across the face with her sodden tail; and another little turn which was well received was when I was filling my syringe with both arms raised and a bullock, backing in alarm from the halter, crashed its craggy behind into my midriff. The wind shot out of me in a sharp hiccup, then the animal decided to turn round in the narrow passage, squashing me like a fly against the railings. I was pop-eyed as it scrambled round; I wondered whether the creaking was coming from my ribs or the wood behind me.

We finished up with the smallest calves and they were just about the most difficult to handle. The shaggy little creatures kicked, bucked, sprang into the air, ran through our legs and even hurtled straight up the walls. Often the brothers had to throw themselves on top of them and bear them to the ground before I could inject them and when the calves felt the needle they stuck out their tongues and bawled deafeningly; outside, the anxious mothers bellowed back in chorus.

It was midday when I reeled out of the buildings. I seemed to have been a month in there, in the suffocating heat, the continuous din, the fusillade of muck.

Frank and George produced a bucket of water and a scrubbing brush and gave me a rough clean-up before I left. A mile from the farm I drove off the unfenced road, got out of the car and dropped down on the cool fell-side. Throwing wide my arms I wriggled my shoulders and my sweat-soaked shirt into the tough grass and let the sweet breeze play over me. With the sun on my face I looked through half closed eyes at the hazy-blue sky.

My ribs ached and I could feel the bruises of a dozen kicks on my legs. I knew I didn't smell so good either. I closed my eyes and grinned at the ridiculous thought that I had been conducting a diagnostic investigation for tuberculosis back there. A strange way to carry out a scientific procedure; a strange way, in fact, to earn a living.

But then I might have been in an office with the windows tight shut against the petrol fumes and the traffic noise, the desk light shining on the columns of figures, my bowler hat hanging on the wall.

Lazily I opened my eyes again and watched a cloud shadow riding over the face of the green hill across the valley. No, no ... I wasn't complaining.

CHAPTER EIGHT

I hardly noticed the passage of the weeks as I rattled along the moorland roads on my daily rounds; but the district was beginning to take shape, the people to emerge as separate personalities. Most days I had a puncture. The tyres were through to the canvas on all wheels; it surprised me that they took me anywhere at all.

One of the few refinements on the car was a rusty 'sunshine roof'. It grated dismally when I slid it back, but most of the time I kept it open and the windows too, and I drove in my shirt sleeves with the delicious air swirling about me. On wet days it didn't help much to close the roof because the rain dripped through the joints and formed pools on my lap and the passenger seat.

I developed great skill in zig-zagging round puddles. To drive through was a mistake as the muddy water fountained up through the gaps in the floor boards.

But it was a fine Summer and long days in the open gave me a tan which rivalled the farmers'. Even mending a puncture was no penance on the high, unfenced roads with the wheeling curlews for company and the wind bringing the scents of flowers and trees up from the valleys. And I could find other excuses to get out and sit on the crisp grass and look out over the airy roof of Yorkshire. It was like taking time out of life. Time to get things into perspective and assess my progress. Everything was so different that it confused me. This countryside after years of city streets, the sense of release from exams and study, the job with its daily challenge. And then there was my boss.

Siegfried Farnon charged round the practice with fierce energy from dawn till dark and I often wondered what drove him on. It wasn't money because he treated it with scant respect. When the bills were paid, the cash went into the pint pot on the mantelpiece and he grabbed handfuls when he wanted it. I never saw him take out a wallet, but his pockets bulged with loose silver and balled-up notes. When he pulled out a thermometer they flew around him in a cloud.

After a week or two of headlong rush he would disappear; maybe for the evening, maybe overnight and often without saying where he was going. Mrs Hall would serve a meal for two, but when she saw I was eating alone she would remove the food without comment.

He dashed off the list of calls each morning with such speed that I was quite often sent hurrying off to the wrong farm or to do the wrong thing. When I told him later of my embarrassment he would laugh heartily.

There was one time when he got involved himself. I had just taken a call from a Mr Heaton of Bronsett about doing a PM on a dead sheep.

'I'd like you to come with me, James,' Siegfried said. 'Things are quiet this morning and I believe they teach you blokes a pretty hot post mortem procedure. I want to see you in action.'

We drove into the village of Bronsett and Siegfried swung the car left into a gated lane.

'Where are you going?' I said. 'Heaton's is at the other end of the village.'

'But you said Seaton's.'

'No, I assure you . . .'

'Look, James, I was right by you when you were talking to the man. I distinctly heard you say the name.'

I opened my mouth to argue further but the car was hurtling down the lane and Siegfried's jaw was jutting. I decided to let him find out for himself.

We arrived outside the farmhouse with a screaming of brakes. Siegfried had left his seat and was rummaging in the boot before the car had stopped shuddering. 'Hell!' he shouted. 'No post mortem knife. Never mind, I'll borrow something from the house.' He slammed down the lid and bustled over to the door.

The farmer's wife answered and Siegfried beamed on her. 'Good morning to you, Mrs Seaton, have you a carving knife?'

The good lady raised her eyebrows. 'What was that you said?'

'A carving knife, Mrs Seaton, a carving knife, and a good sharp one, please.'

'You want a carving knife?'

'Yes, that's right, a carving knife!' Siegfried cried, his scanty store of patience beginning to run out. 'And I wonder if you'd mind hurrying. I haven't much time.'

The bewildered woman withdrew to the kitchen and I could hear whispering and muttering. Children's heads peeped out at intervals to get a quick look at Siegfried stamping irritably on the step. After some delay, one of the daughters advanced timidly, holding out a long, dangerous-looking knife.

Siegfried snatched it from her hand and ran his thumb up and down the edge. 'This is no damn good!' he shouted in exasperation. 'Don't you understand I want something really sharp. Fetch me a steel.'

The girl fled back into the kitchen and there was a low rumble of voices. It was some minutes before another young girl was pushed round the door. She inched her way up to Siegfried, gave him the steel at arm's length and dashed back to safety.

Siegfried prided himself on his skill at sharpening a knife. It was something he enjoyed doing. As he stropped the knife on the steel, he warmed to his work and finally burst into song. There was no sound from the kitchen, only the ring of steel on steel backed by the tuneless singing; there were silent intervals when he carefully tested the edge, then the noise would start again.

When he had completed the job to his satisfaction he peered inside the door. 'Where is your husband?' he called.

There was no reply so he strode into the kitchen, waving the gleaming blade in front of him. I followed him and saw Mrs Seaton and her daughters cowering in the far corner, staring at Siegfried with large, frightened eyes.

He made a sweeping gesture at them with the knife. 'Well, come on, I can get started now!'

'Started what?' the mother whispered, holding her family close to her.

'I want to PM this sheep. You have a dead sheep, haven't you?'

Explanations and apologies followed.

Later, Siegfried remonstrated gravely with me for sending him to the wrong farm.

'You'll have to be a bit more careful in future, James,' he said seriously. 'Creates a very bad impression, that sort of thing.'

Another thing about my new life which interested me was the regular traffic of women through Skeldale House. They were all upper class, mostly beautiful and they had one thing in common – eagerness. They came for drinks, for tea, to dinner, but the real reason was to gaze at Siegfried like parched travellers in the desert sighting an oasis.

I found it damaging to my own ego when their eyes passed over me without recognition or interest and fastened themselves hungrily on my colleague. I wasn't envious, but I was puzzled. I used to study him furtively, trying to fathom the secret of his appeal. Looking at the worn jacket hanging from the thin shoulders, the frayed shirt collar and anonymous tie, I had to conclude that clothes had nothing to do with it.

There was something attractive in the long, bony face and humorous blue eyes, but a lot of the time he was so haggard and sunken-cheeked that I wondered if he was ill.

I often spotted Diana Brompton in the queue and at these times I had to fight down an impulse to dive under the sofa. She was difficult to recognize as the brassy beauty of that afternoon as she looked up meltingly at Siegfried, hanging on his words, giggling like a schoolgirl.

I used to grow cold at the thought that Siegfried might pick her out of the mob and marry her. It worried me a lot because I knew I would have to leave just when I was beginning to enjoy everything about Darrowby.

But Siegfried showed no sign of marrying any of them and the procession continued hopefully. I finally got used to it and stopped worrying.

• • •

I got used, too, to my employer's violent changes of front. There was one morning when Siegfried came down to breakfast, rubbing a hand wearily over red-rimmed eyes.

'Out at 4 AM,' he groaned, buttering his toast listlessly. 'And I don't like to have to say this, James, but it's all your fault.'

'My fault?' I said, startled.

'Yes, lad, your fault. This was a cow with a mild impaction of the rumen. The farmer had been mucking about with it himself for days; a pint of linseed oil one day, a bit of bicarb and ginger the next, and at four o'clock in the morning he decides it is time to call the vet. When I pointed out it could have waited a few hours more he said Mr Herriot told him never to hesitate to ring – he'd come out any hour of the day or night.'

He tapped the top of his egg as though the effort was almost too much for him. 'Well, it's all very well being conscientious and all that, but if a thing has waited several days it can wait till morning. You're spoiling these chaps, James, and I'm getting the backwash of it. I'm sick and tired of being dragged out of my bed for trifles.'

'I'm truly sorry, Siegfried. I honestly had no wish to do that to you. Maybe it's just my inexperience. If I didn't go out, I'd be worried the animal might die. If I left it till morning and it died, how would I feel?'

'That's all right,' snapped Siegfried. 'There's nothing like a dead animal to bring them to their senses. They'll call us out a bit earlier next time.'

I absorbed this bit of advice and tried to act on it. A week later, Siegfried said he wanted a word with me.

'James, I know you won't mind my saying this, but old Sumner was complaining to me today. He says he rang you the other night and you refused to come out to his cow. He's a good client, you know, and a very nice fellow, but he was quite shirty about it. We don't want to lose a chap like that.'

'But it was just a chronic mastitis,' I said. 'A bit of thickening in the milk, that's all. He'd been dosing it himself for nearly a week with some quack remedy. The cow was eating all right, so I thought it would be quite safe to leave it till next day.'

Siegfried put a hand on my shoulder and an excessively patient look spread over his face. I steeled myself. I didn't mind his impatience; I was used to it and could stand it. But the patience was hard to take.

'James,' he said in a gentle voice, 'there is one fundamental rule in our job which transcends all others, and I'll tell you what it is. YOU MUST ATTEND. That is it and it ought to be written on your soul in letters of fire.' He raised a portentous forefinger. 'YOU MUST ATTEND. Always remember that, James; it is the basis of everything. No matter what the circumstances, whether it be wet or fine, night or day, if a client calls you out, you must go; and go cheerfully. You say this didn't sound like an urgent case. Well, after all, you have only the owner's description to guide you and he is not equipped with the knowledge to decide whether it is urgent or not. No, lad, you have to go. Even if they have been treating the animal themselves, it may have taken a turn for the worse. And don't forget,' wagging the finger solmenly 'the animal may die.'

'But I thought you said there was nothing like a dead animal to bring them to their senses,' I said querulously.

'What's that?' barked Siegfried, utterly astonished. 'Never heard such rubbish. Let's have no more of it. Just remember — YOU MUST ATTEND.'

Sometimes he would give me advice on how to live. As when he found me hunched over the phone which I had just crashed down; I was staring at the wall, swearing softly to myself.

Siegfried smiled whimsically. 'Now what is it, James?'

'I've just had a torrid ten minutes with Rolston. You remember that outbreak of calf pneumonia? Well, I spent hours with those calves, poured expensive drugs into them. There wasn't a single death. And now he's complaining about his bill. Not a word of thanks. Hell, there's no justice.'

Siegfried walked over and put his arm round my shoulders. He was wearing his patient look again. 'My dear chap,' he coo'd. 'Just look at you. Red in the face, all tensed up. You mustn't let yourself get upset like this; you must try to relax. Why do you think professional men are cracking up all over the country with coronaries and ulcers? Just because they allow themselves to get all steamed up over piffling little things like you are doing now. Yes, yes, I know these things are annoying, but you've got to take them in your stride. Keep calm, James, calm. It just isn't worth it – I mean, it will all be the same in a hundred years.'

He delivered the sermon with a serene smile, patting my shoulder reassuringly like a psychiatrist soothing a violent patient.

I was writing a label on a jar of red blister a few days later when Siegfried catapulted into the room. He must have kicked the door open because it flew back viciously against the rubber stop and rebounded almost into his face. He rushed over to the desk where I was sitting and began to pound on it with the flat of his hand. His eyes glared wildly from a flushed face.

'I've just come from that bloody swine Holt!' he shouted.

'Ned Holt, you mean?'

'Yes, that's who I mean, damn him!'

I was surprised. Mr Holt was a little man who worked on the roads for the county council. He kept four cows as a sideline and had never been known to pay a veterinary bill; but he was a cheerful character and Siegfried had rendered his unpaid services over the years without objection.

'One of your favourites, isn't he?' I said.

'Was, by God, was,' Siegfried snarled. 'I've been treating Muriel for him. You know, the big red cow second from the far end of his byre. She's had recurrent tympany – coming in from the field every night badly blown – and I'd tried about everything. Nothing did any good. Then it struck me that it might be actinobacillosis of the reticulum. I shot some sodium iodide into the vein and when I saw her today the difference was incredible – she was standing there, chewing her cud, right as rain. I was just patting myself on the back for a smart piece of diagnosis, and do you know what Holt said? He said he knew she'd be better today because last night he gave her half a pound of epsom salts in a bran mash. That was what had cured her.'

Siegfried took some empty cartons and bottles from his pockets and hurled them savagely into the wastepaper basket. He began to shout again.

'Do you know, for the past fortnight I've puzzled and worried and damn nearly dreamt about that cow. Now I've found the cause of the trouble, applied the most modern treatment and the animal has recovered. And what happens? Does the owner express his grateful thanks for my skill? Does he hell – the entire credit goes to the half pound of epsom salts. What I did was a pure waste of time.'

He dealt the desk another sickening blow.

'But I frightened him, James,' he said, his eyes staring, 'By God, I frightened him. When he made that crack about the salts, I yelled out "You bugger!" and made a grab for him. I think I would have strangled him, but he shot into the house and stayed there. I didn't see him again.'

Siegfried threw himself into a chair and began to churn his hair about. 'Epsom salts!' he groaned. 'Oh God, it makes you despair.'

I thought of telling him to relax and pointing out that it would all be the same in a hundred years, but my employer still had an empty serum bottle dangling from one hand. I discarded the idea.

Then there came the day when Siegfried decided to have my car rebored. It had been using a steady two pints of oil a day and he hadn't thought this excessive, but when it got to half a gallon a day he felt something ought to be done. What probably decided him was a farmer on market day saying he always

68

knew when the young vet was coming because he could see the cloud of blue smoke miles away.

When the tiny Austin came back from the garage, Siegfried fussed round it like an old hen. 'Come over here, James,' he called. 'I want to talk to you.'

I saw he was looking patient again and braced myself.

'James,' he said, pacing round the battered vehicle, whisking specks from the paintwork. 'You see this car?'

I nodded.

'Well, it has been rebored, James, rebored at great expense, and that's what I want to talk to you about. You now have in your possession what amounts to a new car.' With an effort he unfastened the catch and the bonnet creaked open in a shower of rust and dirt. He pointed down at the engine, black and oily, with unrelated pieces of flex and rubber tubing hanging around it like garlands. 'You have a piece of fine mechanism here and I want you to treat it with respect. I've seen you belting along like a maniac and it won't do. You've got to nurse this machine for the next two or three thousand miles; thirty miles an hour is quite fast enough. I think it's a crime the way some people abuse a new engine – they should be locked up – so remember, lad, no flogging or I'll be down on you.'

He closed the bonnet with care, gave the cracked windscreen a polish with the cuff of his coat and left.

These strong words made such an impression on me that I crawled round the visits all day almost at walking pace.

The same night, I was getting ready for bed when Siegfried came in. He had two farm lads with him and they both wore silly grins. A powerful smell of beer filled the room.

Siegfried spoke with dignity, slurring his words only slightly. 'James, I met these gentlemen in the Black Bull this evening. We have had several excellent games of dominoes but unfortunately they have missed the last bus. Will you kindly bring the Austin round and I will run them home.'

I drove the car to the front of the house and the farm lads piled in, one in the front, the other in the back. I looked at

Siegfried lowering himself unsteadily into the driving seat and decided to go along. I got into the back.

The two young men lived in a farm far up on the North Moors and, three miles out of the town, we left the main road and our headlights picked out a strip of track twisting along the dark hillside.

Siegfried was in a hurry. He kept his foot on the boards, the note of the engine rose to a tortured scream and the little car hurtled on into the blackness. Hanging on grimly, I leaned forward so that I could shout into my employer's ear. 'Remember this is the car which has just been rebored,' I bellowed above the din.

Siegfried looked round with an indulgent smile. 'Yes, yes, I remember, James. What are you fussing about?' As he spoke, the car shot off the road and bounded over the grass at sixty miles an hour. We all bounced around like corks till he found his way back. Unperturbed, he carried on at the same speed. The silly grins had left the lads' faces and they sat rigid in their seats. Nobody said anything.

The passengers were unloaded at a silent farmhouse and the return journey began. Since it was downhill all the way, Siegfried found he could go even faster. The car leaped and bumped over the uneven surface with its engine whining. We made several brief but tense visits to the surrounding moors, but we got home.

It was a month later that Siegfried had occasion to take his assistant to task once more. 'James, my boy,' he said sorrowfully, 'you are a grand chap, but by God, you're hard on cars. Look at this Austin. Newly rebored a short time ago, in tip top condition, and look at it now – drinking oil. I don't know how you did it in the time. You're a real terror.'

CHAPTER NINE

'First, please,' I called as I looked into the waiting room. There was an old lady with a cat in a cardboard box, two small boys trying to keep hold of a rabbit, and somebody I didn't recognize at first. Then I remembered – it was Soames.

When it was his turn, he came into the surgery but he was a vastly different character from the one I knew. He wore an ingratiating smile. His head bobbed up and down as he spoke. He radiated anxiety to please. And the most interesting thing was that his right eye was puffed and closed and surrounded by an extensive area of bluish-black flesh.

'I hope you don't mind my coming to see you, Mr Herriot,' he said. 'The fact is I have resigned my position with his lordship and am looking for another post. I was wondering if you and Mr Farnon would put in a word for me if you heard of anything.'

I was too astonished at the transformation to say much. I replied that we would do what we could and Soames thanked me effusively and bowed himself out.

I turned to Siegfried after he had gone. 'Well, what do you make of that?'

'Oh, I know all about it.' Siegfried looked at me with a wry smile. 'Remember I told you he was working one or two shady sidelines up there – selling a few bags of corn or a hundred-weight of fertilizer here and there. It all mounted up. But it didn't last; he got a bit careless and he was out on his ear before he knew what had happened.'

'And how about the lovely black eye?'

'Oh, he got that from Tommy. You must have seen Tommy when you were there. He's the horseman.'

My mind went back to that uncomfortable night and to the

quiet man holding the horse's head. 'I remember him – big fat chap.'

'Yes, he's a big lad and I'd hate to have him punch me in the eye. Soames gave him a hell of a life and as soon as Tommy heard about the sacking he paid a visit just to settle the score.'

I was now comfortably settled into the way of life in Skeldale House. At first I wondered where Tristan fitted into the set up. Was he supposed to be seeing practice, having a holiday, working or what? But it soon became clear that he was a factotum who dispensed and delivered medicines, washed the cars, answered the phone and even, in an emergency, went to a case.

At least, that was how Siegfried saw him and he had a repertoire of tricks aimed at keeping him on his toes. Like returning unexpectedly or bursting into a room in the hope of catching him doing nothing. He never seemed to notice the obvious fact that the college vacation was over and Tristan should have been back there. I came to the conclusion over the next few months that Tristan must have had some flexible arrangement with the college authorities because, for a student, he seemed to spend a surprising amount of time at home.

He interpreted his role rather differently from his brother and, while resident in Darrowby, he devoted a considerable amount of his acute intelligence to the cause of doing as little as possible. Tristan did, in fact, spend much of his time sleeping in a chair. When he was left behind to dispense when we went out on our rounds he followed an unvarying procedure. He half filled a sixteen ounce bottle with water, added a few drachms of chlorodyne and a little epicacuanha, pushed the cork in and took it through to the sitting-room to stand by his favourite chair. It was a wonderful chair for his purpose; old fashioned and high backed with wings to support the head.

He would get out his *Daily Mirror*, light a Woodbine and settle down till sleep overcame him. If Siegfried rushed in on him he grabbed the bottle and started to shake it madly, inspecting the contents at intervals. Then he went through to the dispensary, filled up the bottle and labelled it.

It was a sound, workable system but it had one big snag. He never knew whether it was Siegfried or not when the door opened and often I walked in and found him half lying in his chair, staring up with startled, sleep-blurred eyes while he agitated his bottle.

Most evenings found him sitting on a high stool at the bar counter of the Drovers' Arms, conversing effortlessly with the barmaid. At other times he would be out with one of the young nurses from the local hospital which he seemed to regard as an agency to provide him with female company. All in all, he managed to lead a fairly full life.

Saturday night, 10.30 PM and I was writing up my visits when the phone rang. I swore, crossed my fingers and lifted the receiver.

'Hello, Herriot speaking.'

'Oh, it's you is it,' growled a dour voice in broadest Yorkshire. 'Well, ah want Mr Farnon.'

'I'm sorry, Mr Farnon is out. Can I help you?'

'Well, I 'ope so, but I'd far raither 'ave your boss. This is Sims of Beal Close.'

(Oh no, please no, not Beal Close on a Saturday night. Miles up in the hills at the end of a rough lane with about eight gates.)

'Yes, Mr Sims, and what is the trouble?'

'Ah'll tell you, there is some trouble an' all. I 'ave a grand big show 'oss here. All of seventeen hands. He's cut 'isself badly on the hind leg, just above the hock. I want him stitched immediately.'

(Glory be! Above the hock! What a charming place to have to stitch a horse. Unless he's very quiet, this is going to be a real picnic.)

'How big is the wound, Mr Sims?'

'Big? It's a gurt big thing about a foot long and bleedin''

73

like 'ell. And this 'oss is as wick as an eel. Could kick a fly's eye out. Ah can't get near 'im nohow. Goes straight up wall when he sees anybody. By gaw, I tell you I had 'im to t'black-smith t'other day and feller was dead scared of 'im. Twiltin' gurt 'oss 'e is.'

(Damn you, Mr Sims, damn Beal Close and damn your twiltin' gurt 'oss.)

'Well, I'll be along straight away. Try to have some men handy just in case we have to throw him.'

'Throw 'im? Throw 'im? You'd never throw this 'oss. He'd kill yer first. Anyways, I 'ave no men here so you'll have to manage on your own. Ah know Mr Farnon wouldn't want a lot of men to help 'im.'

(Oh lovely, lovely. This is going to be one for the diary.)

'Very well, I'm leaving now, Mr Sims.'

'Oh, ah nearly forgot. My road got washed away in the floods yesterday. You'll 'ave to walk the last mile and a half. So get a move on and don't keep me waiting all night.'

(This is just a bit much.)

'Look here, Mr Sims, I don't like your tone. I said I would leave now and I will get there just as soon as I can.'

'You don't like ma tone, eh? Well, ah don't like useless young apprentices practising on my good stock, so ah don't want no cheek from you. You know nowt about t'damn job, any road.'

(That finally does it.)

'Now just listen to me, Sims. If it wasn't for the sake of the horse I'd refuse to come out at all. Who do you think you are, anyway? If you ever try to speak to me like that again . . .'

'Now, now, Jim, get a grip on yourself. Take it easy old boy. You'll burst a blood vessel if you go on like this.'

'Who the devil . . .?'

'Ah, ah, Jim, calm yourself now. That temper of yours, you know. You'll really have to watch it.'

'Tristan! Where the hell are you speaking from?'

'The kiosk outside the Drovers. Five pints inside me and feeling a bit puckish. Thought I'd give you a ring.'

'By God, I'll murder you one of these days if you don't stop this game. It's putting years on me. Now and again isn't so bad, but this is the third time this week.'

'Ah, but this was by far the best, Jim. It was really wonderful. When you started drawing yourself up to your full height – it nearly killed me. Oh God, I wish you could have heard yourself.' He trailed off into helpless laughter.

And then my feeble attempts at retaliation; creeping, trembling, into some lonely phone box.

'Is that young Mr Farnon?' in a guttural croak. 'Well, this is Tilson of High Woods. Ah want you to come out here immediately I 'ave a terrible case of . . .'

'Excuse me for interrupting, Jim, but is there something the matter with your tonsils? Oh, good. Well, go on with what you were saying, old lad. Sounds very interesting.'

There was only one time when I was not on the receiving end. It was Tuesday – my half day – and at 11.30 AM a call came in. An eversion of the uterus in a cow. This is the tough job in country practice and I felt the usual chill.

It happens when the cow, after calving, continues to strain until it pushes the entire uterus out and it hangs down as far as the animal's hocks. It is a vast organ and desperately difficult to replace, mainly because the cow, having once got rid of it, doesn't want it back. And in a straightforward contest between man and beast the odds were very much on the cow.

The old practitioners, in an effort to even things up a bit, used to sling the cow up by its hind limbs and the more inventive among them came up with all sorts of contraptions like the uterine valise which was supposed to squeeze the organ into smaller bulk. But the result was usually the same – hours of back-breaking work.

The introduction of the epidural anaesthetic made everything easier by removing sensation from the uterus and preventing the cow from straining but, for all that, the words 'calf bed out' coming over the line were guaranteed to wipe the smile off any vet's face.

I decided to take Tristan in case I needed a few pounds of extra push. He came along but showed little enthusiasm for the idea. He showed still less when he saw the patient, a very fat shorthorn lying, quite unconcerned, in her stall. Behind her, a bloody mass of uterus, afterbirth, muck and straw spilled over into the channel.

She wasn't at all keen to get up, but after we had done a bit of shouting and pushing at her shoulder she rose to her feet, looking bored.

The epidural space was difficult to find among the rolls of fat and I wasn't sure if I had injected all the anaesthetic into the right place. I removed the afterbirth, cleaned the uterus and placed it on a clean sheet held by the farmer and his brother. They were frail men and it was all they could do to keep the sheet level. I wouldn't be able to count on them to help me much.

I nodded to Tristan; we stripped off our shirts, tied clean sacks round our waists and gathered the uterus in our arms.

It was badly engorged and swollen and it took us just an hour to get it back. There was a long spell at the beginning when we made no progress at all and the whole idea of pushing the enormous organ through a small hole seemed ludicrous, like trying to thread a needle with a sausage. Then there was a few minutes when we thought we were doing famously only to find we were feeding the thing down through a tear in the sheet, (Siegfried once told me he had spent half a morning trying to stuff a uterus up a cow's rectum. What really worried him, he said, was that he nearly succeeded) and at the end when hope was fading, there was the blissful moment when the whole thing began to slip inside and incredibly disappeared from sight.

Somewhere halfway through we both took a breather at

76

the same time and stood panting, our faces almost touching. Tristan's cheeks were prettily patterned where a spouting artery had sprayed him; I was able to look deep into his eyes and I read there a deep distaste for the whole business.

Lathering myself in the bucket and feeling the ache in my shoulders and back, I looked over at Tristan. He was pulling his shirt over his head as though it cost him the last of his strength. The cow, chewing contentedly at a mouthful of hay, had come best out of the affair.

Out in the car, Tristan groaned. 'I'm sure that sort of thing isn't good for me. I feel as though I've been run over by a steam roller. Hell, what a life this is at times.'

After lunch I rose from the table. 'I'm off to Brawton now, Triss, and I think I'd better mention that you may not have seen the last of that cow. These bad cases sometimes recur and there's a chance that little lot may come out again. If it does, it's all yours because Siegfried won't be back for hours and nothing is going to stop me having my half day.'

For once Tristan's sense of humour failed him. He became haggard, he seemed to age suddenly. 'Oh God,' he moaned, 'don't even talk about it. I'm all in – another session like that would kill me. And on my own! It would be the end of me, I tell you.'

'Ah well,' I said sadistically, 'try not to worry. It may never happen.'

It was when I saw the phone box about ten miles along the Brawton road that the thought struck me. I slowed down and got out of the car. 'I wonder,' I muttered, 'I wonder if I could do it just once.'

Inside the box, inspiration was strong in me. I wrapped my handkerchief over the mouthpiece, dialled the practice number and when I heard Tristan on the line I shouted at the top of my voice. 'Are you t'young feller that put our cow's calf bed back this morning?'

'Yes, I'm one of them.' Tension sprang into Tristan's voice. 'Why, is there something wrong?'

77

'Aye, there is summat wrong,' I bawled. 'She's putten it out again.'

'Out again? Out again? All of it?' He was almost screaming.

'Aye, it's a terrible mess. Pourin' blood and about twice size it was this morning. You'll 'ave some job with 'er.'

There was a long silence and I wondered if he had fainted. Then I heard him again, hoarse but resolute. 'Very well, I'll come straight away.'

There was another pause then he spoke again almost in a whisper. 'Is it out completely?'

I broke down then. There was a wistful quality about the words which defeated me; a hint of a wild hope that the farmer may have been exaggerating and that there might be only a tiny piece peeping out. I began to laugh. I would have liked to toy with my victim a little longer but it was impossible. I laughed louder and took my handkerchief from the mouthpiece so that Tristan could hear me.

I listened for a few seconds to the frenzied swearing at the other end then gently replaced the receiver. It would probably never happen again but it was sweet, very sweet.

CHAPTER TEN

'You want Mr Herriot? Certainly, I'll get him for you.' Siegfried cupped the phone with his hand. 'Come on, James, here's another one prefers you to me.' I glanced at him quickly, but he was smiling. He was pleased.

I thought, as I took the phone, of the tales I had heard of the other kind of boss; the man who couldn't bear to be knocked off his little pedestal. And I thought, too, of the difference a few weeks had made in the farmers' attitude; they didn't look past me now, hoping that Mr Farnon had come with me. They were beginning to accept me, and I liked to think that it wasn't only their hospitable traditions that made them ask me in for a 'bit o' dinner'.

This really meant something, because, with the passage of time, an appreciation of the Dales people had grown in me; a sense of the value of their carefully given friendship. The higher up the country, the more I liked them. At the bottom of the valley, where it widened into the plain, the farmers were like farmers everywhere, but the people grew more interesting as the land heightened, and in the scattered hamlets and isolated farms near the bleak tops I found their characteristics most marked; their simplicity and dignity, their rugged independence and their hospitality.

This Sunday morning it was the Bellerbys and they lived at the top of Halden, a little valley branching off the main Dale. My car bumped and rattled over the last rough mile of an earth road with the tops of boulders sticking up every few yards.

I got out and from where I stood, high at the head, I could see all of the strangely formed cleft in the hills, its steep sides grooved and furrowed by countless streams feeding the boisterous Halden Beck which tumbled over its rocky bed far below. Down there, were trees and some cultivated fields, but immediately behind me the wild country came crowding in on the bowl where the farmhouse lay. Halsten Pike, Alstang, Birnside – the huge fells with their barbarous names were very near.

Up here, the trappings of civilization seemed far away. The farm buildings had been built massively of stone hundreds of years ago with the simple object of sheltering the animals. Those ancient masons were untroubled by regulations about the light and ventilation and the cow byre was gloomy, thick walled, almost windowless. The floor was broken and pitted, and rotting wooden partitions separated the cows from each other.

I went in, groping my way until my eyes grew accustomed to the dim light. There was nobody there but a roan cow had a label tied to its tail. Since this was a common way of communicating with the vet I lifted the tail and read 'Felon, back quarters'.

I pushed the cow over and began to examine the back teats. I was drawing out the stringy, discoloured milk when a voice addressed me from the doorway: 'Oh, it's you, Mr Herriot. I'm right glad you've come to see us this morning. You could do us such a great favour if you would.'

I looked up and saw Ruth Bellerby, a fine looking woman in her late thirties. She was the go-ahead member of the family and had an intelligent, questing mind. She was a great believer in self-improvement for the Dales people.

'I'll be glad to help you if I can, Miss Bellerby. What is it you'd like me to do?'

'Well, Mr Herriot, you know they are putting on the Messiah at Darrowby church this afternoon and we did badly want to go, but it's such a job getting the pony and trap ready and it's so slow. If you could give us a lift down in your car, I know we'd be able to get a ride back. It would be such a help.'

'Of course I'll run you down,' I replied. 'I'll be delighted to do it. I'm going myself as a matter of fact. You don't get many chances to hear good music in Darrowby.'

It was good to have a chance to help these kindly people. I had always marvelled at the Bellerbys. They seemed to me to be survivors from another age and their world had a timeless quality. They were never in a hurry; they rose when it was light, went to bed when they were tired, ate when they were hungry and seldom looked at a clock.

Ruth led the way over to the house. 'There's just mother and dad and me going. Bob's not interested, I'm afraid.'

I was slightly taken aback when I entered the house. The family were just sitting down to Sunday dinner and were still in their working clothes. I stole a look at my watch; a quarter to twelve and the performance started at 2 PM. Oh well, I probably had plenty of time.

'Come on, young man,' said little Mr Bellerby. 'Sit down and have a bit o' dinner.'

It was always a bit tricky refusing these invitations without causing offence, but I pointed out that my own meal would be ready when I got back and it would be hard on Mrs Hall if it were wasted.

They were quick to appreciate this argument and settled down round the scrubbed kitchen table. Mrs Bellerby served a large, round Yorkshire pudding to each of them and poured a pool of gravy into it from a quart size enamel jug. I had had a hard morning and the delicious scent that rose from the gravy as it ran over the golden slabs was a sweet torture. But I consoled myself with the thought that the fact of my sitting there would make them hurry.

The pudding was consumed in leisurely silence, then Bob, an amiable, thick-set youth in his twenties, pushed out his empty plate. He did not say anything, but his mother planked down another pudding on the plate and plied the gravy jug again. His parents and sister watched him benevolently as he methodically demolished the thick, doughy mass.

Next, a tremendous roast appeared from the oven and Mr Bellerby hacked and sawed at it till they all had a heap of thick slices on their plates. Then mountains of mashed potatoes were served from something that looked like a washing-up bowl. Chopped turnip followed and the family went into action again.

There was no sign of haste. They ate calmly and quietly without any small talk. Bob had an extra helping of mashed potatoes.

The Bellerbys were relaxed and happy, but I couldn't say the same about myself. Hunger was tearing fiercely at me and the minutes on my watch were ticking away relentlessly.

There was a decent interval before Mrs Bellerby went over to the old fire oven in the corner, opened the door and pulled forth a great flat baking tin of steaming apple pie. She then proceeded to carve off about a square foot for each of them and deluged it with something like a pint of custard from another towering enamel jug.

The family set to as though they were just beginning the meal and once more a busy silence fell on the group. Bob cleared his plate in effortless style and pushed it wordlessly into the middle of the table. His mother was ready with another great rectangle of pie and another copious libation of custard.

It was going to be a close thing, I thought, but this surely must be the end. They would realize time was getting short and start to change. But, to my consternation, Mrs Bellerby moved slowly over to the fire and put the kettle on, while her husband and Bob pushed their chairs back and stretched out their legs. They both wore corduroy breeches with the lacing undone and on their feet were enormous hobnailed boots. Bob, after a search through his pockets, brought out a battered packet of cigarettes and lay back in a happy coma as his mother put a cup of tea in front of him. Mr Bellerby produced a clasp knife and began to cut up some plug tobacco for his pipe.

As they rearranged themselves round the table and began to slowly sip the hot tea, I found I had started to exhibit all the classical symptoms of tension. Pounding pulse, tighly clenched jaws and the beginnings of a headache.

After a second cup of tea, there were signs of activity. Mr Bellerby rose with a groan, scratched his shirt front and stretched luxuriously. 'Well, young man, we'll just have a bit of a wash and get changed. Bob'll stay and talk to you – he's not coming with us.'

There was a lot of splashing and spluttering in the big stone sink at the far end of the kitchen as they made their ablutions, then they disappeared upstairs. I was greatly relieved to find that it didn't take them long to change. Mr Bellerby was down very soon, transformed in appearance by a stiff and shiny suit of navy blue serge with a faint greenish tinge. His wife and daughter followed soon in a blaze of flowered cotton.

'Ah well, now, here we are. All ready, eh?' There was a note of hysteria in my heartiness. 'Right, then, off we go. After you, ladies.'

But Ruth did not move. She was pulling on a pair of white gloves and looking at her brother sprawled in his chair. 'You know, Bob, you're nowt but a disgrace!' she burst out. 'Here we are going off to hear this lovely music and you're lying there in your muck, not caring. You've no interest in culture at all. You care no more about bettering yourself than one of them bullocks out there.'

Bob stirred uneasily under this sudden attack, but there was more to come.

Ruth stamped her foot. 'Really, it makes my blood boil to look at you. And I know we won't be right out of t'door before you're asleep. Aye, snoring there all afternoon like a pig.' She swung round to Mrs Bellerby. 'Mother! I've made up my mind. I'm not going to leave him snoring here. He's got to come with us!'

I felt the sweat start out on my brow. I began to babble. 'But don't you think, perhaps . . . might be just a little late . . . starts at two o'clock . . . my lunch . . .'

But my words were utterly lost. Ruth had the bit properly between her teeth. 'Get up out of there, Bob! Get up this minute and get dressed!' She shut her mouth tightly and thrust out her lower jaw.

She was too much for Bob. Although an impressive eater, he didn't seem to have much mind of his own. He mumbled sulkily and shuffled over to the sink. He took off his shirt and they all sat down and watched as he lathered his torso with a large block of White Windsor and sluiced his head and neck by working the pump handle by the side of the sink.

The family regarded him happily, pleased that he was coming with them and content in the knowledge that it would be good for him. Ruth watched his splashings with the light of love in her eyes. She kept looking over at me as if to say 'Isn't this grand'.

For my part, I was only just stopping myself from tearing out

83

my hair in great handfuls. A compulsion to leap up and pace the floor, to scream at the top of my voice showed that I was nearing the end of my tether. I fought this feeling by closing my eyes and I must have kept them closed for a long time because, when I opened them, Bob was standing by my side in a suit exactly like his father's.

I could never remember much about that ride to Darrowby. I had only a vague recollection of the car hurtling down the stony track at forty miles an hour. Of myself staring straight ahead with protruding eyes and the family, tightly packed but cheerful, thoroughly enjoying the ride.

Even the imperturbable Mrs Hall was a little tight lipped as I shot into the house at ten to two and out again at two after bolting her good food.

I was late for the Messiah. The music had started as I crept into the church and I ran a gauntlet of disapproving stares. Out of the corner of my eye I saw the Bellerbys sitting very upright, all in a row. It seemed to me that they looked disapproving, too.

CHAPTER ELEVEN

I looked again at the slip of paper where I had written my visits. 'Dean, 3, Thompson's Yard. Old dog ill.'

There were a lot of these 'yards' in Darrowby. They were, in fact, tiny streets, like pictures from a Dickens' novel. Some of them opened off the market place and many more were scattered behind the main thoroughfares in the old part of the town. From the outside you could see only an archway and it was always a surprise to me to go down a narrow passage and come suddenly upon the uneven rows of little houses with no two alike, looking into each other's windows across eight feet of cobbles.

In front of some of the houses a strip of garden had been dug out and marigolds and nasturtiums straggled over the rough stones; but at the far end the houses were in a tumble-down condition and some were abandoned with their windows boarded up.

Number three was down at this end and looked as though it wouldn't be able to hold out much longer.

The flakes of paint quivered on the rotten wood of the door as I knocked; above, the outer wall bulged dangerously on either side of a long crack in the masonry.

A small, white haired man answered. His face, pinched and lined, was enlivened by a pair of cheerful eyes; he wore a much-darned woollen cardigan, patched trousers and slippers.

'I've come to see your dog,' I said, and the old man smiled.

'Oh, I'm glad you've come, sir,' he said. 'I'm getting a bit worried about the old chap. Come inside, please.'

He led me into the tiny living-room. 'I'm alone now, sir. Lost my missus over a year ago. She used to think the world of the old dog.'

The grim evidence of poverty was everywhere. In the worn out lino, the fireless hearth, the dank, musty smell of the place. The wall paper hung away from the damp patches and on the table the old man's solitary dinner was laid; a fragment of bacon, a few fried potatoes and a cup of tea. This was life on the old age pension.

In the corner, on a blanket, lay my patient, a cross-bred labrador. He must have been a big, powerful dog in his time, but the signs of age showed in the white hairs round his muzzle and the pale opacity in the depth of his eyes. He lay quietly and looked at me without hostility.

'Getting on a bit, isn't he, Mr Dean?'

'Aye he is that. Nearly fourteen, but he's been like a pup galloping about until these last few weeks. Wonderful dog for his age, is old Bob and he's never offered to bite anybody in his life. Children can do anything with him. He's my only friend now – I hope you'll soon be able to put him right.'

'Is he off his food, Mr Dean?'

'Yes, clean off, and that's a strange thing because by gum, he could eat. He always sat by me and put his head on my knee at meal times, but he hasn't been doing it lately.'

I looked at the dog with growing uneasiness. The abdomen was grossly distended and I could read the tell-tale symptoms of pain; the catch in the respirations, the retracted commissures of the lips, the anxious, preoccupied expression in the eyes.

When his master spoke, the tail thumped twice on the blankets and a momentary interest showed in the white old eyes; but it quickly disappeared and the blank, inward look returned.

I passed my hand carefully over the dog's abdomen. Ascites was pronounced and the dropsical fluid had gathered till the pressure was intense. 'Come on, old chap,' I said, 'Let's see if we can roll you over.' The dog made no resistance as I eased him slowly on to his other side, but, just as the movement was completed, he whimpered and looked round. The cause of the trouble was now only too easy to find.

I palpated gently. Through the thin muscle of the flank I could feel a hard, corrugated mass; certainly a splenic or hepatic carcinoma, enormous and completely inoperable. I stroked the old dog's head as I tried to collect my thoughts. This wasn't going to be easy.

'Is he going to be ill for long?' the old man asked, and again came the thump, thump of the tail at the sound of the loved voice. 'It's miserable when Bob isn't following me round the house when I'm doing my little jobs.'

'I'm sorry, Mr Dean, but I'm afraid this is something very serious. You see this large swelling. It is caused by an internal growth.'

'You mean . . . cancer?' the little man said faintly.

'I'm afraid so, and it has progressed too far for anything to be done. I wish there was something I could do to help him, but there isn't.'

The old man looked bewildered and his lips trembled. 'Then he's going to die?'

86

I swallowed hard. 'We really can't just leave him to die, can we? He's in some distress now, but it will soon be an awful lot worse. Don't you think it would be kindest to put him to sleep? After all, he's had a good, long innings.' I always aimed at a brisk, matter-of-fact approach, but the old clichés had an empty ring.

The old man was silent, then he said, 'Just a minute,' and slowly and painfully knelt down by the side of the dog. He did not speak, but ran his hand again and again over the grey old muzzle and the ears, while the tail thump, thump, thumped on the floor.

He knelt there a long time while I stood in the cheerless room, my eyes taking in the faded pictures on the walls, the frayed, grimy curtains, the broken-springed arm chair.

At length the old man struggled to his feet and gulped once or twice. Without looking at me, he said huskily, 'All right, will you do it now?'

I filled the syringe and said the things I always said. 'You needn't worry, this is absolutely painless. Just an overdose of an anaesthetic. It is really an easy way out for the old fellow.'

The dog did not move as the needle was inserted, and, as the barbiturate began to flow into the vein, the anxious expression left his face and the muscles began to relax. By the time the injection was finished, the breathing had stopped.

'Is that it?' the old man whispered.

'Yes, that's it,' I said. 'He is out of his pain now.'

The old man stood motionless except for the clasping and unclasping of his hands. When he turned to face me his eyes were bright. 'That's right, we couldn't let him suffer, and I'm grateful for what you've done. And now, what do I owe you for your services, sir?'

'Oh, that's all right, Mr Dean,' I said quickly. 'It's nothing – nothing at all. I was passing right by here – it was no trouble.'

The old man was astonished. 'But you can't do that for nothing.'

'Now please say no more about it, Mr Dean. As I told you, I

was passing right by your door.' I said goodbye and went out of the house, through the passage and into the street. In the bustle of people and the bright sunshine, I could still see only the stark, little room, the old man and his dead dog.

As I walked towards my car, I heard a shout behind me. The old man was shuffling excitedly towards me in his slippers. His cheeks were streaked and wet, but he was smiling. In his hand he held a small, brown object.

'You've been very kind, sir. I've got something for you.' He held out the object and I looked at it. It was tattered but just recognizable as a precious relic of a bygone celebration.

'Go on, it's for you,' said the old man. 'Have a cigar.'

CHAPTER TWELVE

It was unfortunate that Siegfried ever had the idea of delegating the book-keeping to his brother, because Skeldale House had been passing through a period of peace and I found it soothing.

For nearly a fortnight there had been hardly a raised voice or an angry word except for one unpleasant interlude when Siegfried had come in and found his brother cycling along the passage. Tristan found all the rage and shouting quite incomprehensible – he had been given the job of setting the table and it was a long way from kitchen to dining-room; it seemed the most natural thing in the world to bring his bike in.

Autumn had come with a sharpness in the air and at nights the log fire burned bright in the big room, sending shadows flickering over the graceful alcoves and up to the high, carved ceiling. It was always a good time when the work of the day was through and the three of us lay back in the shabby arm chairs and stretched our feet out to the blaze.

Tristan was occupied with the *Daily Telegraph* crossword which he did every night. Siegfried was reading and I was dozing. It embarrassed me to be drawn into the crossword; Siegfried could usually make a contribution after a minute's thought but Tristan could have the whole thing worked out while I wrestled with the first clue.

The carpet round our feet was hidden by the dogs, all five of them, draped over each other in heavy-breathing layers and adding to the atmosphere of camaraderie and content.

It seemed to me that a chill breath struck through the comfort of the room as Siegfried spoke. 'Market day tomorrow and the bills have just gone out. They'll be queueing up to give us their money so I want you, Tristan, to devote the entire day to taking it from them. James and I are going to be busy, so you'll be in sole charge. All you have to do is take their cheques, give them a receipt and enter their names in the receipt book. Now do you think you can manage that without making a bloody hash of it?'

I winced. It was the first discordant note for a long time and it struck deep.

'I think I might just about cope with that,' Tristan replied haughtily.

'Good. Let's get to bed then.'

But, next day, it was easy to see that the assignment was right up Tristan's street. Stationed behind the desk, he took in the money in handfuls; and all the time he talked. But he did not talk at random; each character got a personal approach.

With the upright methodist, it was the weather, the price of cows and the activities of the village institute. The raffish type with his cap on one side, exhaling fumes of market ale, got the latest stories which Tristan kept on the backs of envelopes. But with the ladies he rose to his greatest heights. They were on his side from the first because of his innocent, boyish face, and when he turned the full blast of his charm on them their surrender was complete.

I was amazed at the giggles which came from behind the door. I was pleased the lad was doing well. Nothing was going wrong this time.

Tristan was smug at lunch time and cock-a-hoop at tea. Siegfried too, was satisfied with the day's takings which his brother presented in the form of a column of neat figures accurately totalled at the bottom. 'Thank you, Tristan, very efficient.' All was sweetness.

At the end of the day I was in the yard, throwing the used bottles from the boot of my car into a bin. It had been a busy day and I had accumulated a bigger than usual load of empties.

Tristan came panting in from the garden. 'Jim, I've lost the receipt book!'

'Always trying to pull my leg, always joking,' I said, 'Why don't you give your sense of humour a rest some time?' I laughed heartily and sent a liniment bottle crashing among the others.

He plucked at my sleeve. 'I'm not joking, Jim, believe me. I really have lost the bloody thing.' For once, his *sang froid* had deserted him. His eyes were wide, his face pale.

'But it can't just have disappeared,' I said. 'It's bound to turn up.'

'It'll never turn up.' Tristan wrung his hands and did a bit of pacing on the cobbles. 'Do you know I've spent about two hours searching for it. I've ransacked the house. It's gone, I tell you.'

'But it doesn't matter, does it? You'll have transferred all the names into the ledger.'

'That's just it. I haven't. I was going to do it tonight.'

'So that means that all the farmers who have been handing you money today are going to get the same bill next month?'

'Looks like it. I can't remember the names of more than two or three of them.'

I sat down heavily on the stone trough. 'Then God help us all, especially you. These Yorkshire lads don't like parting with their brass once, but when you ask them to do it twice – oh, brother!'

Another thought struck me and I said with a touch of cruelty. 'And how about Siegfried. Have you told him yet?'

A spasm crossed Tristan's face. 'No, he's just come in. I'm going to do it now.' He squared his shoulders and strode from the yard.

I decided not to follow him to the house. I didn't feel strong enough for the scene which was bound to follow. Instead, I went out into the back lane and round behind the house to the market place where the lighted entrance of the Drovers' Arms beckoned in the dusk.

I was sitting behind a pint when Tristan came in looking as though somebody had just drained half a gallon of blood from him.

'How did it go?' I asked.

'Oh, the usual, you know. Bit worse this time, maybe. But I can tell you this, Jim. I'm not looking forward to a month from today.'

The receipt book was never found and, a month later, all the bills were sent out again, timed, as usual, to arrive on market day morning.

The practice was quiet that particular day and I had finished my round by mid morning. I didn't go into the house, because through the waiting room window I could see rows of farmers sitting round the walls; they all wore the same offended, self-righteous expression.

I stole away to the market place. When I had time, I enjoyed moving among the stalls which crowded the ancient square. You could buy fruit, fish, second-hand books, cheeses, clothes, in fact nearly everything; but the china stall was my favourite.

It was run by a Jewish gentleman from Leeds – fat, confident, sweating, and with a hypnotic selling technique. I never got tired of watching him. He fascinated me. He was in his best form today, standing in a little clearing surrounded on all sides by heaps of crockery, while beyond, the farmers' wives listened open-mouthed to his oratory.

'Ah'm not good lookin',' he was saying. 'Ah'm not clever,

but by God ah can talk. Ah can talk the hind leg off a donkey. Now look 'ere.' He lifted a cheap cup and held it aloft, but tenderly, gripping it between his thick thumb and forefinger, his little finger daintily outspread. 'Beautiful, isn't it? Now isn't that lovely?' Then he placed it reverently on the palm of his hand and displayed it to the audience. 'Now I tell you ladies, you can buy this self same tea-set in Conners in Bradford for three pounds fifteen. I'm not jokin' nor jestin', it's there and that's the price. But my price, ladies?' and here he fished out an old walking stick with a splintered handle. 'My price for this beautiful tea-set?' He held the stick by its end and brought it crashing down on an empty tea-chest. 'Never mind three pound fifteen.' Crash! 'Never mind three pound.' Crash! 'Never mind two pound.' Crash! 'Never mind thirty bob.' Crash! ''ere, 'ere, come on, who'll give me a quid?' Not a soul moved. 'All right, all right, I can see ah've met me match today. Go on, seventeen and a tanner the lot.' A final devastating crash and the ladies began to make signals and fumble in their handbags. A little man emerged from the back of the stall and started to hand out the tea-sets. The ritual had been observed and everybody was happy.

I was waiting, deeply content, for the next item from the virtuoso when I saw a burly figure in a check cap waving wildly at me from the edge of the crowd. He had his hand inside his jacket and I knew what he was feeling for. I didn't hesitate but dodged quickly behind a stall laden with pig troughs and wire netting. I had gone only a few steps before another farmer hailed me purposefully. He was brandishing an envelope.

I felt trapped, then I saw a way of escape. Rapidly skirting a counter displaying cheap jewellery, I plunged into the doorway of the Drovers' Arms and, avoiding the bar which was full of farmers, slipped into the manager's office. I was safe; this was one place where I was always welcome.

The manager looked up from his desk, but he did not smile. 'Look here,' he said sharply, 'I brought my dog in to see you some time ago and in due course I received an account from

92

you.' I cringed inwardly. 'I paid by return and was extremely surprised this morning to find that another account had been rendered. I have here a receipt signed by . . .'

I couldn't stand any more. 'I'm very sorry, Mr Brooke, but there's been a mistake. I'll put it right. Please accept our apologies.'

This became a familiar refrain over the next few days, but it was Siegfried who had the most unfortunate experience. It was in the bar of his favourite pub, the Black Swan. He was approached by Billy Breckenridge, a friendly, jocular little character, one of Darrowby's worthies. 'Hey, remember that three and six I paid at your surgery? I've had another bill for it.'

Siegfried made a polished apology – he'd had a lot of practice – and bought the man a drink. They parted on good terms.

The pity of it was that Siegfried, who seldom remembered anything, didn't remember this. A month later, also in the Swan, he ran into Billy Breckenridge again. This time, Billy wasn't so jocular. 'Hey, remember that bill you sent me twice? Well, I've had it again.'

Siegfried did his best, but his charm bounced off the little man. He was offended. 'Right, I can see you don't believe I paid your bill. I had a receipt from your brother, but I've lost it.' He brushed aside Siegfried's protestations. 'No, no, there's only one way to settle this. I say I've paid the three and six, you say I haven't. All right, I'll toss you for it.'

Miserably, Siegfried demurred, but Billy was adamant. He produced a penny and, with great dignity, balanced it on his thumbnail. 'OK, you call.'

'Heads,' muttered Siegfried and heads it was. The little man did not change expression. Still dignified, he handed the three and six to Siegfried. 'Perhaps we might be able to consider the matter closed.' He walked out of the bar.

Now there are all kinds of bad memories, but Siegfried's was of the inspired type. He somehow forgot to make a note of this last transaction and, at the end of the month, Billy Brenckenridge received a fourth request for the amount which he had already paid twice. It was about then that Siegfried changed his pub and started going to the Cross Keys.

CHAPTER THIRTEEN

As Autumn wore into Winter and the high tops were streaked with the first snows, the discomforts of practice in the Dales began to make themselves felt.

Driving for hours with frozen feet, climbing to the high barns in biting winds which seared and flattened the wiry hill grass. The interminable stripping off in draughty buildings and the washing of hands and chest in buckets of cold water, using scrubbing soap and often a piece of sacking for a towel.

I really found out the meaning of chapped hands. When there was a rush of work, my hands were never quite dry and the little red fissures crept up almost to my elbows.

This was when some small animal work came as a blessed relief. To step out of the rough, hard routine for a while; to walk into a warm drawing-room instead of a cow house and tackle something less formidable than a horse or a bull. And among all those comfortable drawing-rooms there was none so beguiling as Mrs Pumphrey's.

Mrs Pumphrey was an elderly widow. Her late husband, a beer baron whose breweries and pubs were scattered widely over the broad bosom of Yorkshire, had left her a vast fortune and a beautiful house on the outskirts of Darrowby. Here she lived with a large staff of servants, a gardener, a chauffeur and Tricki Woo. Tricki Woo was a Pekingese and the apple of his mistress' eye.

Standing now in the magnificent doorway, I furtively rubbed the toes of my shoes on the backs of my trousers and blew on my cold hands. I could almost see the deep armchair drawn close to the leaping flames, the tray of cocktail biscuits, the bottle of excellent sherry. Because of the sherry, I was always careful to time my visits for half an hour before lunch.

A maid answered my ring, beaming on me as an honoured guest and led me to the room, crammed with expensive furniture and littered with glossy magazines and the latest novels. Mrs Pumphrey, in the high backed chair by the fire, put down her book with a cry of delight. 'Trick! Tricki! Here is your uncle Herriot.' I had been made an uncle very early and, sensing the advantages of the relationship, had made no objection.

Tricki, as always, bounded from his cushion, leaped on to the back of a sofa and put his paws on my shoulders. He then licked my face thoroughly before retiring, exhausted. He was soon exhausted because he was given roughly twice the amount of food needed for a dog of his size. And it was the wrong kind of food.

'Oh, Mr Herriot,' Mrs Pumphrey said, looking at her pet anxiously. 'I'm so glad you've come. Tricki has gone flop-bott again.'

This ailment, not to be found in any text book, was her way of describing the symptoms of Tricki's impacted anal glands. When the glands filled up, he showed discomfort by sitting down suddenly in mid walk and his mistress would rush to the phone in great agitation.

'Mr Herriot! Please come, he's going flop-bott again!'

I hoisted the little dog on to a table and, by pressure on the anus with a pad of cotton wool, I evacuated the glands.

It baffled me that the Peke was always so pleased to see me. Any dog who could still like a man who grabbed him and squeezed his bottom hard every time they met had to have an incredibly forgiving nature. But Tricki never showed any resentment; in fact he was an outstandingly equable little animal, bursting with intelligence, and I was genuinely attached to him. It was a pleasure to be his personal physician.

The squeezing over, I lifted my patient from the table, noticing the increased weight, the padding of extra flesh over the ribs. 'You know, Mrs Pumphrey, you're overfeeding him again.

Didn't I tell you to cut out all those pieces of cake and give him more protein?'

'Oh yes, Mr Herriot,' Mrs Pumphrey wailed. 'But what can I do? He's so tired of chicken.'

I shrugged; it was hopeless. I allowed the maid to lead me to the palatial bathroom where I always performed a ritual handwashing after the operation. It was a huge room with a fully stocked dressing table, massive green ware and rows of glass shelves laden with toilet preparations. My private guest towel was laid out next to the slab of expensive soap.

Then I returned to the drawing-room, my sherry glass was filled and I settled down by the fire to listen to Mrs Pumphrey. It couldn't be called a conversation because she did all the talking, but I always found it rewarding.

Mrs Pumphrey was likeable, gave widely to charities and would help anybody in trouble. She was intelligent and amusing and had a lot of waffling charm; but most people have a blind spot and her's was Tricki Woo. The tales she told about her darling ranged far into the realms of fantasy and I waited eagerly for the next instalment.

'Oh Mr Herriot, I have the most exciting news. Tricki has a pen pal! Yes, he wrote a letter to the editor of *Doggy World* enclosing a donation, and told him that even though he was descended from a long line of Chinese emperors, he had decided to come down and mingle freely with the common dogs. He asked the editor to seek out a pen pal for him among the dogs he knew so that they could correspond to their mutual benefit. And for this purpose, Tricki said he would adopt the name of Mr Utterbunkum. And, do you know, he received the most beautiful letter from the editor' (I could imagine the sensible man leaping upon this potential gold mine) 'who said he would like to introduce Bonzo Fotheringham, a lonely Dalmatian who would be delighted to exchange letters with a new friend in Yorkshire.'

I sipped the sherry. Tricki snored on my lap. Mrs Pumphrey went on.

'But I'm so disappointed about the new Summerhouse – you know I got it specially for Tricki so we could sit out together on warm afternoons. It's such a nice little rustic shelter, but he's taken a passionate dislike to it. Simply loathes it – absolutely refuses to go inside. You should see the dreadful expression on his face when he looks at it. And do you know what he called it yesterday? Oh, I hardly dare tell you.' She looked around the room before leaning over and whispering: 'He called it "the bloody hut"!'

The maid struck fresh life into the fire and refilled my glass. The wind hurled a handful of sleet against the window. This, I thought, was the life. I listened for more.

'And did I tell you, Mr Herriot, Tricki had another good win yesterday? You know, I'm sure he must study the racing columns, he's such a tremendous judge of form. Well, he told me to back Canny Lad in the three o'clock at Redcar yesterday and, as usual, it won. He put on a shilling each way and got back nine shillings.'

These bets were always placed in the name of Tricki Woo and I thought with compassion of the reactions of the local bookies. The Darrowby turf accountants were a harassed and fugitive body of men. A board would appear at the end of some alley urging the population to invest with Joe Downs and enjoy perfect security. Joe would live for a few months on a knife edge while he pitted his wits against the knowledgeable citizens, but the end was always the same; a few favourites would win in a row and Joe would be gone in the night, taking his board with him. Once I had asked a local inhabitant about the sudden departure of one of these luckless nomads. He replied unemotionally: 'Oh, we brok 'im.'

Losing a regular flow of shillings to a dog must have been a heavy cross for these unfortunate men to bear.

'I had such a frightening experience last week,' Mrs Pumphrey continued. 'I was sure I would have to call you out. Poor little Tricki – he went completely crackerdog!'

97

I mentally lined this up with flop-bott among the new canine diseases and asked for more information.

'It was awful. I was terrified. The gardener was throwing rings for Tricki – you know he does this for half an hour every day.' I had witnessed this spectacle several times. Hodgkin, a dour, bent old Yorkshireman who looked as though he hated all dogs and Tricki in particular, had to go out on the lawn every day and throw little rubber rings over and over again. Tricki bounded after them and brought them back, barking madly till the process was repeated. The bitter lines on the old man's face deepened as the game progressed. His lips moved continually, but it was impossible to hear what he was saying.

Mrs Pumphrey went on: 'Well, he was playing his game, and he does adore it so, when suddenly, without warning, he went crackerdog. He forgot all about his rings and began to run around in circles, barking and yelping in such a strange way. Then he fell over on his side and lay like a little dead thing. Do you know, Mr Herriot, I really thought he was dead, he lay so perfectly still. And what hurt me most was that Hodgkin began to laugh. He has been with me for twenty-four years and I have never even seen him smile, and yet, when he looked down at that still form, he broke into a queer, high-pitched cackle. It was horrid. I was just going to rush to the telephone when Tricki got up and walked away – he seemed perfectly normal.'

Hysteria, I thought, brought on by wrong feeding and over-excitement. I put down my glass and fixed Mrs Pumphrey with a severe glare. 'Now look, this is just what I was talking about. If you persist in feeding all that fancy rubbish to Tricki you are going to ruin his health. You really must get him on to a sensible dog diet of one or, at the most, two small meals a day of meat and brown bread or a little biscuit. And nothing in between.'

Mrs Pumphrey shrank into her chair, a picture of abject guilt. 'Oh, please don't speak to me like that. I do try to give him the right things, but it is so difficult. When he begs for his little titbits. I can't refuse him.' She dabbed her eyes with a handkerchief.

But I was unrelenting. 'All right, Mrs Pumphrey, it's up to you, but I warn you that if you go on as you are doing, Tricki will go crackerdog more and more often.'

I left the cosy haven with reluctance, pausing on the gravelled drive to look back at Mrs Pumphrey waving and Tricki, as always, standing against the window, his wide-mouthed face apparently in the middle of a hearty laugh.

Driving home, I mused on the many advantages of being Tricki's uncle. When he went to the seaside he sent me boxes of oak-smoked kippers; and when the tomatoes ripened in his greenhouse, he sent a pound or two every week. Tins of tobacco arrived regularly, sometimes with a photograph carrying a loving inscription.

But it was when the Christmas hamper arrived from Fortnum and Mason's that I decided that I was on a really good thing which should be helped along a bit. Hitherto, I had merely rung up and thanked Mrs Pumphrey for the gifts, and she had been rather cool, pointing out that it was Tricki who had sent the things and he was the one who should be thanked.

With the arrival of the hamper it came to me, blindingly, that I had been guilty of a grave error of tactics. I set myself to compose a letter to Tricki. Avoiding Siegfried's sardonic eye, I thanked my doggy nephew for his Christmas gifts and for all his generosity in the past. I expressed my sincere hopes that the festive fare had not upset his delicate digestion and suggested that if he did experience any discomfort he should have recourse to the black powder his uncle always prescribed. A vague feeling of professional shame was easily swamped by floating visions of kippers, tomatoes and hampers. I addressed the envelope to Master Tricki Pumphrey, Barlby Grange and slipped it into the post box with only a slight feeling of guilt.

On my next visit, Mrs Pumphrey drew me to one side. 'Mr Herriot,' she whispered, 'Tricki adored your charming letter and he will keep it always, but he was very put out about one thing – you addressed it to Master Tricki and he does insist upon Mister. He was dreadfully affronted at first, quite beside himself, but when he saw it was from you he soon recovered his good temper. I can't think why he should have these little prejudices. Perhaps it is because he is an only dog – I do think an only dog develops more prejudices than one from a large family.'

Entering Skeldale House was like returning to a colder world. Siegfried bumped into me in the passage. 'Ah, who have we here? Why I do believe it's dear Uncle Herriot. And what have you been doing, Uncle? Slaving away at Barlby Grange, I' expect. Poor fellow, you must be tired out. Do you really think it's worth it, working your fingers to the bone for another hamper?'

CHAPTER FOURTEEN

Looking back, I can scarcely believe we used to spend all those hours in making up medicines. But our drugs didn't come to us in proprietary packages and before we could get out on the road we had to fill our cars with a wide variety of carefully compounded and largely useless remedies.

When Siegfried came upon me that morning I was holding a twelve ounce bottle at eye level while I poured syrup of coccilana into it. Tristan was moodily mixing stomach powders with a mortar and pestle and he stepped up his speed of stroke when he saw his brother's eye on him. He was surrounded by packets of the powder and, further along the bench, were orderly piles of pessaries which he had made by filling cellophane cylinders with boric acid.

Tristan looked industrious; his elbow jogged furiously as he ground away at the ammon carb and nux vomica. Siegfried smiled benevolently.

I smiled too. I felt the strain badly when the brothers were at variance, but I could see that this was going to be one of the happy mornings. There had been a distinct improvement in the atmosphere since Christmas when Tristan had slipped casually back to college and, apparently without having done any work, had re-sat and passed his exams. And there was something else about my boss today; he seemed to glow with inner satisfaction as though he knew for certain that something good was on the way. He came in and closed the door.

'I've got a bit of good news.'

I screwed the cork into the bottle. 'Well, don't keep us in suspense. Let's have it.'

Siegfried looked from one of us to the other. He was almost smirking. 'You remember that bloody awful shambles when Tristan took charge of the bills?'

His brother looked away and began to grind still faster, but Siegfried laid a friendly hand on his shoulder. 'No, don't worry, I'm not going to ask you to do it again. In fact, you'll never have to do it again because, from now on, the job will be done by an expert.' He paused and cleared his throat. 'We're going to have a secretary.'

As we stared blankly at him he went on. 'Yes, I picked her myself and I consider she's perfect.'

'Well, what's she like?' I asked.

Siegfried pursed his lips. 'It's difficult to describe her. But just think – what do we want here? We don't want some flighty young thing hanging about the place. We don't want a pretty little blonde sitting behind that desk powdering her nose and making eyes at everybody.'

'We don't?' Tristan interrupted, plainly puzzled.

'No, we don't!' Siegfried rounded on him. 'She'd be daydreaming about her boy friends half the time and just when we'd got her trained to our ways she'd be running off to get married.'

Tristan still looked unconvinced and it seemed to exasperate his brother. Siegfried's face reddened. 'And there's another thing. How could we have an attractive young girl in here with somebody like you in the house. You'd never leave her alone.'

Tristan was nettled. 'How about you?'

'I'm talking about you, not me!' Siegfried roared. I closed my eyes. The peace hadn't lasted long. I decided to cut in. 'All right, tell us about the new secretary.'

With an effort, he mastered his emotion. 'Well, she's in her fifties and she has retired after thirty years with Green and Moulton in Bradford. She was company secretary there and I've had the most wonderful reference from the firm. They say she is a model of efficiency and that's what we want in this practice – efficiency. We're far too slack. It's just a stroke of luck for us that she decided to come and live in Darrowby. Anyway, you'll be able to meet her in a few minutes – she's coming at ten o'clock this morning.'

The church clock was chiming when the door bell rang. Siegfried hastened out to answer it and led his great discovery into the room in triumph. 'Gentlemen, I want you to meet Miss Harbottle.'

She was a big, high-bosomed woman with a round healthy face and gold-rimmed spectacles. A mass of curls, incongruous and very dark, peeped from under her hat; they looked as if they might be dyed and they didn't go with her severe clothes and brogue shoes.

It occurred to me that we wouldn't have to worry about her rushing off to get married. It wasn't that she was ugly, but she had a jutting chin and an air of effortless command that would send any man running for his life.

I shook hands and was astonished at the power of Miss Harbottle's grip. We looked into each other's eyes and had a friendly trial of strength for a few seconds, then she seemed happy to call it a draw and turned away. Tristan was entirely unprepared and a look of alarm spread over his face as his hand was engulfed; he was released only when his knees started to buckle.

She began a tour of the office while Siegfried hovered behind her, rubbing his hands and looking like a shopwalker with his favourite customer. She paused at the desk, heaped high with in-coming and out-going bills, Ministry of Agriculture forms, circulars from drug firms with here and there stray boxes of pills and tubes of udder ointment.

Stirring distastefully among the mess, she extracted the dog-eared old ledger and held it up between finger and thumb. 'What's this?'

Siegfried trotted forward. 'Oh, that's our ledger. We enter the visits into it from our day book which is here somewhere.' He scrabbled about on the desk. 'Ah, here it is. This is where we write the calls as they come in.'

She studied the two books for a few minutes with an expression of amazement which gave way to a grim humour. 'You gentlemen will have to learn to write if I am going to look after your books. There are three different hands here, but this one is by far the worst. Quite dreadful. Whose is it?'

She pointed to an entry which consisted of a long, broken line with an occasional undulation.

'That's mine, actually,' said Siegfried, shuffling his feet. 'Must have been in a hurry that day.'

'But it's all like that, Mr Farnon. Look here and here and here. It won't do, you know.'

Siegfried put his hands behind his back and hung his head.

'I expect you keep your stationery and envelopes in here.' She pulled open a drawer in the desk. It appeared to be filled entirely with old seed packets, many of which had burst open. A few peas and french beans rolled gently from the top of the heap. The next drawer was crammed tightly with soiled calving ropes which somebody had forgotten to wash. They didn't smell so good and Miss Harbottle drew back hurriedly; but she was not easily deterred and tugged hopefully at the third drawer. It came open with a musical clinking and she looked down on a dusty row of empty pale ale bottles.

She straightened up slowly and spoke patiently. 'And where, may I ask, is your cash box?'

'Well, we just stuff it in there, you know.' Siegfried pointed to the pint pot on the corner of the mantelpiece. 'Haven't got what you'd call a proper cash box, but this does the job all right.'

Miss Harbottle looked at the pot with horror. 'You just stuff . . .' Crumpled cheques and notes peeped over the brim at her; many of their companions had burst out on to the hearth below. 'And you mean to say that you go out and leave that money there day after day?'

'Never seems to come to any harm,' Siegfried replied.

'And how about your petty cash?'

Siegfried gave an uneasy giggle. 'All in there, you know. All cash – petty and otherwise.'

Miss Harbottle's ruddy face had lost some of its colour 'Really, Mr Farnon, this is too bad. I don't know how you have gone on so long like this. I simply do not know. However, I'm confident I will be able to straighten things out very soon. There is obviously nothing complicated about your business – a simple card index system would be the thing for your accounts. The other little things,' – she glanced back unbelieving at the pot – 'I will put right very quickly.'

'Fine, Miss Harbottle, fine.' Siegfried was rubbing his hands harder than ever. 'We'll expect you on Monday morning.'

'Nine o'clock sharp, Mr Farnon.'

After she had gone there was a silence. Tristan had enjoyed her visit and was smiling thoughtfully, but I felt uncertain.

'You know, Siegfried,' I said, 'maybe she is a demon of efficiency but isn't she just a bit tough?'

'Tough?' Siegfried gave a loud, rather cracked laugh. 'Not a bit of it. You leave her to me. I can handle her.'

CHAPTER FIFTEEN

There was little furniture in the dining-room but the noble lines and the very size of the place lent grace to the long sideboard and the modest mahogany table where Tristan and I sat at breakfast.

The single large window was patterned with frost and in the street outside, the footsteps of the passers-by crunched in the crisp snow. I looked up from my boiled egg as a car drew up. There was a stamping in the porch, the outer door banged shut and Siegfried burst into the room. Without a word he made for the fire and hung over it, leaning his elbows on the grey marble mantelpiece. He was muffled almost to the eyes in greatcoat and scarf but what you could see of his face was purplish blue.

He turned a pair of streaming eyes to the table. 'A milk fever up at old Heseltine's. One of the high buildings. God, it was cold up there. I could hardly breathe.'

As he pulled off his gloves and shook his numbed fingers in front of the flames, he darted sidelong glances at his brother. Tristan's chair was nearest the fire and he was enjoying his breakfast as he enjoyed everything, slapping the butter happily on to his toast and whistling as he applied the marmalade. His *Daily Mirror* was balanced against the coffee pot. You could almost see the waves of comfort and contentment coming from him.

Siegfried dragged himself unwillingly from the fire and dropped into a chair. 'I'll just have a cup of coffee, James. Heseltine was very kind – asked me to sit down and have breakfast with him. He gave me a lovely slice of home fed bacon – a bit fat, maybe, but what a flavour! I can taste it now.'

He put down his cup with a clatter. 'You know, there's no

reason why we should have to go to the grocer for our bacon and eggs. There's a perfectly good hen house at the bottom of the garden and a pig sty in the yard with a boiler for the swill. All our household waste could go towards feeding a pig. We'd probably do it quite cheaply.'

He rounded on Tristan who had just lit a Woodbine and was shaking out his *Mirror* with the air of ineffable pleasure which was peculiar to him. 'And it would be a useful job for you. You're not producing much sitting around here on your arse all day. A bit of stock keeping would do you good.'

Tristan put down his paper as though the charm had gone out of it. 'Stock keeping? Well, I feed your mare as it is.' He didn't enjoy looking after Siegfried's new hunter because every time he turned her out to water in the yard she would take a playful kick at him in passing.

Siegfried jumped up. 'I know you do, and it doesn't take all day, does it? It won't kill you to take on the hens and pigs.'

'Pigs?' Tristan looked startled. 'I thought you said pig?'

'Yes, pigs. I've just been thinking. If I buy a litter of weaners we can sell the others and keep one for ourselves. Won't cost a thing that way.'

'Not with free labour, certainly.'

'Labour? Labour? You don't know what it means! Look at you lying back there puffing your head off. You smoke too many of those bloody cigarettes!'

'So do you.'

'Never mind me, I'm talking about you!' Siegfried shouted.

I got up from the table with a sigh. Another day had begun.

When Siegfried got an idea he didn't muck about. Immediate action was his watchword. Within forty-eight hours a litter of ten little pigs had taken up residence in the sty and twelve Light Sussex pullets were pecking about behind the wire of the hen house. He was particularly pleased with the pullets. 'Look at them, James; just on point of lay and a very good strain, too. There'll be just a trickle of eggs at first, but once they get cracking we'll be snowed under. Nothing like a nice fresh egg warm from the nest.'

It was plain from the first that Tristan didn't share his brother's enthusiasm for the hens. I often found him hanging about outside the hen house, looking bored and occasionally throwing bread crusts over the wire. There was no evidence of the regular feeding, the balanced diet recommended by the experts. As egg producers, the hens held no appeal for him, but he did become mildly interested in them as personalities. An odd way of clucking, a peculiarity in gait – these things amused him.

But there were no eggs and as the weeks passed, Siegfried became increasingly irritable. 'Wait till I see the chap that sold me those hens. Damned scoundrel. Good laying strain my foot!' It was pathetic to see him anxiously exploring the empty nesting boxes every morning.

One afternoon, I was going down the garden when Tristan called to me. 'Come over here, Jim. This is something new. I bet you've never seen anything like it before.' He pointed upwards and I saw a group of unusually coloured large birds perched in the branches of the elms. There were more of them in the neighbour's apple trees.

I stared in astonishment. 'You're right, I've never seen anything like them. What are they?'

'Oh, come on,' said Tristan, grinning in delight, 'surely there's something familiar about them. Take another look.'

I peered upwards again. 'No, I've never seen birds as big as that and with such exotic plumage. What is it – a freak migration?'

Tristan gave a shout of laughter. 'They're our hens!'

'How the devil did they get up there?'

'They've left home. Hopped it.'

'But I can only see seven. Where are the rest of them?'

'God knows. Let's have a look over the wall.'

The crumbling mortar gave plenty of toe holds between the bricks and we looked down into the next garden. The other five hens were there, pecking contentedly among some cabbages.

It took a long time to get them all back into the hen house and the tedious business had to be repeated several times a day thereafter. For the hens had clearly grown tired of life under Tristan and decided that they would do better living off the country. They became nomads, ranging ever further afield in their search for sustenance.

At first the neighbours chuckled. They phoned to say their children were rounding up the hens and would we come and get them; but with the passage of time their jocularity wore thin. Finally Siegfried was involved in some painful interviews. His hens, he was told, were an unmitigated nuisance.

It was after one particularly unpleasant session that Siegfried decided that the hens must go. It was a bitter blow and as usual he vented his fury on Tristan. 'I must have been mad to think that any hens under your care would ever lay eggs. But really, isn't it just a bit hard? I give you this simple little job and one would have thought that even you would be hard put to it to make a mess of it. But look at the situation after only three weeks. Not one solitary egg have we seen. The bloody hens are flying about the countryside like pigeons. We are permanently estranged from our neighbours. You've done a thorough job haven't you?' All the frustrated egg producer in Siegfried welled out in his shrill tones.

Tristan's expression registered only wounded virtue, but he was rash enough to try to defend himself. 'You know, I thought there was something queer about those hens from the start,' he muttered.

Siegfried shed the last vestiges of his self control. 'Queer!' he yelled wildly. 'You're the one that's queer, not the poor bloody hens. You're the queerest bugger there is. For God's sake get out – get out of my sight!'

Tristan withdrew with quiet dignity.

It took some time for the last echoes of the poultry venture to die away but after a fortnight, sitting again at the dining-table with Tristan, I felt sure that all was forgotten. So that it was with a strange sense of the workings of fate that I saw Siegfried stride into the room and lean menacingly over his brother. 'You remember those hens, I suppose,' he said almost in a whisper, 'you'll recall that I gave them away to Mrs Dale, that old aged pensioner down Brown's Yard. Well, I've just been speaking to her. She's delighted with them. Gives them a hot mash night and morning and she's collecting ten eggs a day.' His voice rose almost to a scream. 'Ten eggs, do you hear, ten eggs!'

I hurriedly swallowed the last of my tea and excused myself. I trotted along the passage out the back door and up the garden to my car. On the way I passed the empty hen house. It had a forlorn look. It was a long way to the dining-room but I could still hear Siegfried.

CHAPTER SIXTEEN

'Jim! Come over here and look at these little beggars.' Tristan laughed excitedly as he leaned over the door of the pig sty.

I walked across the yard. 'What is it?'

'I've just given them their swill and it's a bit hot. Just look at them!'

The little pigs were seizing the food, dropping it and walking suspiciously round it. Then they would creep up, touch the hot potatoes with their muzzles and leap back in alarm. There was none of the usual meal time slobbering; just a puzzled grunting.

Right from the start Tristan had found the pigs more interesting than the hens which was a good thing because he had to retrieve himself after the poultry disaster. He spent a lot of time in the yard, sometimes feeding or mucking out but more often resting his elbows on the door watching his charges.

As with the hens, he was more interested in their characters than their ability to produce pork or bacon. After he poured the swill into the long trough he always watched, entranced, while the pigs made their first rush. Soon, in the desperate gobbling there would be signs of uneasiness. The tiny animals would begin to glance sideways till their urge to find out what their mates were enjoying so much became unbearable; they would start to change position frantically, climbing over each other's backs and falling into the swill.

Old Boardman was a willing collaborator, but mainly in an advisory capacity. Like all countrymen he considered he knew all about the husbandry and diseases of animals and, it turned out, pigs were his speciality. There were long conferences in the dark room under the Bairnsfather cartoons and the old man grew animated over his descriptions of the vast, beautiful animals he had reared in that very sty.

Tristan listened with respect because he had solid proof of Boardman's expertise in the way he handled the old brick boiler. Tristan could light the thing but it went out if he turned his back on it; but it was docile in Boardman's hands. I often saw Tristan listening wonderingly to the steady blub-blub while the old man rambled on and the delicious scent of cooking pig potatoes drifted over them both.

But no animal converts food more quickly into flesh than a pig and as the weeks passed the little pink creatures changed with alarming speed into ten solid, no-nonsense porkers. Their characters deteriorated, too. They lost all their charm. Meal times stopped being fun and became a battle with the odds growing heavier against Tristan all the time.

I could see that it brought a lot of colour into old Boardman's life and he always dropped whatever he was doing when he saw Tristan scooping the swill from the boiler.

He obviously enjoyed watching the daily contest from his seat on the stone trough. Tristan bracing himself, listening to the pigs squealing at the rattle of the bucket; giving a few fearsome shouts to encourage himself then shooting the bolt and plunging among the grunting, jostling animals; broad, greedy snouts forcing into the bucket, sharp feet grinding his toes, heavy bodies thrusting against his legs.

I couldn't help smiling when I remembered the light-hearted game it used to be. There was no laughter now. Tristan finally took to brandishing a heavy stick at the pigs before he dared to go in. Once inside his only hope of staying on his feet was to clear a little space by beating on the backs.

It was on a market day when the pigs had almost reached bacon weight that I came upon Tristan sprawled in his favourite chair. But there was something unusual about him; he wasn't asleep, no medicine bottle, no Woodbines, no *Daily Mirror*. His arms hung limply over the sides of the chair, his eyes were half closed and sweat glistened on his forehead.

'Jim,' he whispered. 'I've had the most hellish afternoon I've ever had in my life.'

I was alarmed at his appearance. 'What's happened.'

'The pigs,' he croaked. 'They escaped today.'

'Escaped! How the devil could they do that?'

Tristan tugged at his hair. 'It was when I was feeding the mare. I gave her her hay and thought I might as well feed the pigs at the same time. You know what they've been like lately – well, today they went berserk. Soon as I opened the door they charged out in a solid block. Sent me up in the air, bucket and all, then ran over the top of me.' He shuddered and looked up at me wide-eyed. 'I'll tell you this, Jim, when I was lying there on the cobbles, covered with swill and that lot trampling on me, I thought it was all over. But they didn't savage me. They belted out through the yard door at full gallop.'

'The yard door was open then?'

'Too true it was. I would just choose this one day to leave it open.'

Tristan sat up and wrung his hands. 'Well, you know, I thought it was all right at first. You see, they slowed down when they got into the lane and trotted quietly round into the front street with Boardman and I hard on their heels. They formed a group there. Didn't seem to know where to go next. I was sure we were going to be able to head them off, but just then one of them caught sight of itself in Robson's shop window.'

He gave a remarkable impression of a pig staring at its reflection for a few moments then leaping back with a startled grunt.

'Well, that did it, Jim. The bloody animal panicked and shot off into the market place at about fifty miles an hour with the rest after it.'

I gasped. Ten large pigs loose among the packed stalls and market day crowds was difficult even to imagine.

'Oh God, you should have seen it.' Tristan fell back wearily into his chair. 'Women and kids screaming. The stall holders, police and everybody else cursing me. There was a terrific traffic jam too – miles of cars tooting like hell while the policeman on point duty concentrated on browbeating me.' He wiped his brow. 'You know that fast talking merchant on the china stall – well, today I saw him at a loss for words. He was balancing a cup on his palm and in full cry when one of the pigs got its fore feet on his stall and stared him straight in the face. He stopped as if he'd been shot. Any other time it would have been funny but I thought the perishing animal was going to wreck the stall. The counter was beginning to rock when the pig changed its mind and made off.'

'What's the position now?' I asked. 'Have you got them back?'

'I've got nine of them back,' Tristan replied, leaning back and closing his eyes. 'With the help of almost the entire male population of the district I've got nine of them back. The tenth was last seen heading North at a good pace. God knows where it is now. Oh, I didn't tell you – one of them got into the post office. Spent quite some time in there.' He put his hands over his face. 'I'm for it this time, Jim. I'll be in the hands of the law after this lot. There's no doubt about it.'

I leaned over and slapped his leg. 'Oh, I shouldn't worry. I don't suppose there's been any serious damage done.'

Tristan replied with a groan. 'But there's something else. When I finally closed the door after getting the pigs back in their sty I was on the verge of collapse. I was leaning against the wall gasping for breath when I saw the mare had gone. Yes, gone. I'd gone straight out after the pigs and forgot to close her box. I don't know where she is. Boardman said he'd look around – I haven't the strength.'

Tristan lit a trembling Woodbine. 'This is the end, Jim. Siegfried will have no mercy this time.'

As he spoke, the door flew open and his brother rushed in. 'What the hell is going on?' he roared. 'I've just been speaking to the vicar and he says my mare is in his garden eating his wallflowers. He's hopping mad and I don't blame him. Go on, you lazy scoundrel. Don't lie there, get over to the vicarage this instant and bring her back!'

Tristan did not stir. He lay inert, looking up at his brother. His lips moved feebly.

'No,' he said.

'What's that?' Siegfried shouted incredulously. 'Get out of that chair immediately. Go and get that mare!'

'No,' replied Tristan.

I felt a chill of horror. This sort of mutiny was unprecedented. Siegfried had gone very red in the face and I steeled myself for an eruption; but it was Tristan who spoke.

'If you want your mare you can get her yourself.' His voice was quiet with no note of defiance. He had the air of a man to whom the future is of no account.

Even Siegfried could see that this was one time when Tristan had had enough. After glaring down at his brother for a few seconds he turned and walked. He got the mare himself.

Nothing more was said about the incident but the pigs were moved hurriedly to the bacon factory and were never replaced. The stock keeping project was at an end.

CHAPTER SEVENTEEN

When I came in, Miss Harbottle was sitting, head bowed, over the empty cash box; she looked bereaved. It was a new, shiny, black box with the words 'Petty Cash' printed on top in white letters. Inside was a red book with the incomings and outgoings recorded in neat columns. But there was no money.

Miss Harbottle's sturdy shoulders sagged. She listlessly took up the red book between finger and thumb and a lonely sixpence rolled from between its pages and tinkled into the box. 'He's been at it again,' she whispered.

A stealthy footstep sounded in the passage. 'Mr Farnon!' she called out. And to me: 'It's really absurd the way the man always tries to slink past the door.'

Siegfried shuffled in. He was carrying a stomach tube and pump, calcium bottles bulged from his jacket pockets and a bloodless castrator dangled from the other hand.

He smiled cheerfully but I could see he was uncomfortable, not only because of the load he carried, but because of his poor tactical position. Miss Harbottle had arranged her desk across the corner diagonally opposite the door and he had to walk across a long stretch of carpet to reach her. From her point of view it was strategically perfect. From her corner she could see every inch of the big room, into the passage when the door was open and out on to the front street from the window on her left. Nothing escaped her – it was a position of power.

Siegfried looked down at the square figure behind the desk. 'Good morning, Miss Harbottle, can I do anything for you?'

The grey eyes glinted behind the gold-rimmed spectacles. 'You can, indeed, Mr Farnon. You can explain why you have once more emptied my petty cash box.'

'Oh, I'm so sorry. I had to rush through to Brawton last night and I found myself a bit short. There was really nowhere else to turn to.'

'But Mr Farnon, in the two months I have been here, we must have been over this a dozen times. What is the good of my trying to keep an accurate record of the money in the practice if you keep stealing it and spending it?'

'Well, I suppose I got into the habit in the old pint pot days. It wasn't a bad system, really.'

'It wasn't a system at all. It was anarchy. You cannot run a business that way. But I've told you this so many times and each time you have promised to alter your ways. I feel almost at my wits' end.'

'Oh, never mind, Miss Harbottle. Get some more out of the bank and put it in your box. That'll put it right.' Siegfried gathered up the loose coils of the stomach tube from the floor and turned to go, but Miss Harbottle cleared her throat warningly.

'There are one or two other matters. Will you please try to keep your other promise to enter your visits in the book every day and to price them as you do so. Nearly a week has gone by since you wrote anything in. How can I possibly get the bills out on the first of the month? This is most important, but how do you expect me to do it when you impede me like this?'

'Yes, yes, I'm sorry, but I have a string of calls waiting. I really must go.' He was halfway across the floor and the tube was uncoiling itself again when he heard the ominous throat clearing behind him.

'And one more thing, Mr Farnon. I still can't decipher your writing. These medical terms are difficult enough, so please take a little care and don't scribble.'

'Very well, Miss Harbottle.' He quickened his pace through the door and into the passage where, it seemed, was safety and peace. He was clattering thankfully over the tiles when the familiar rumbling reached him. She could project that sound a surprising distance by giving it a bit of extra pressure, and it was a summons which had to be obeyed. I could hear him wearily putting the tube and pump on the floor; the calcium bottles must have been digging into his ribs because I heard them go down too.

He presented himself again before the desk. Miss Harbottle wagged a finger at him. 'While I have you here I'd like to mention another point which troubles me. Look at this day book. You see all these slips sticking out of the pages? They are all queries – there must be scores of them – and I am at a standstill until you clear them for me. When I ask you you never have the time. Can you go over them with me now?'

Siegfried backed away hurriedly. 'No, no, not just now. As I said, I have some urgent calls waiting. I'm very sorry but it will have to be some other time. First chance I get I'll come in and see you.' He felt the door behind him and with a last glance at the massive, disapproving figure behind the desk, he turned and fled.

CHAPTER EIGHTEEN

I could look back now on six months of hard practical experience. I had treated cows, horses, pigs, dogs and cats seven days a week; in the morning, afternoon, evening and through the hours when the world was asleep. I had calved cows and farrowed sows till my arms ached and the skin peeled off. I had been knocked down, trampled on and sprayed liberally with every kind of muck. I had seen a fair cross section of the diseases of animals. And yet a little voice had begun to niggle at the back of my mind; it said I knew nothing, nothing at all.

This was strange, because those six months had been built upon five years of theory; a slow, painful assimilation of thousands of facts and a careful storage of fragments of knowledge like a squirrel with its nuts. Beginning with the study of plants and the lowest forms of life, working up to dissection in the anatomy lab and physiology and the vast, soul-less territory of materia medica. Then pathology which tore down the curtain of ignorance and let me look for the first time into the deep secrets. And parasitology, the teeming other world of the worms and fleas and mange mites. Finally, medicine and surgery, the crystallization of my learning and its application to the everyday troubles of animals.

And there were many others, like physics, chemistry, hygiene; they didn't seem to have missed a thing. Why then should I feel I knew nothing? Why had I begun to feel like an astronomer looking through a telescope at an unknown galaxy? This sensation that I was only groping about on the fringes of limitless space was depressing. It was a funny thing, because everybody else seemed to know all about sick animals. The chap who held the cow's tail, the neighbour from the next farm, men in pubs, jobbing gardeners; they all knew and were free and confident with their advice.

I tried to think back over my life. Was there any time when I had felt this supreme faith in my own knowledge. And then I remembered.

I was back in Scotland, I was seventeen and I was walking under the arch of the Veterinary College into Montrose Street. I had been a student for three days but not until this afternoon had I felt the thrill of fulfilment. Messing about with botany and zoology was all right but this afternoon had been the real thing; I had had my first lecture in animal husbandry.

The subject had been the points of the horse. Professor Grant had hung up a life size picture of a horse and gone over it from nose to tail, indicating the withers, the stifle, the hock, the poll and all the other rich, equine terms. And the professor had been wise; to make his lecture more interesting he kept throwing in little practical points like 'This is where we find curb,' or 'Here is the site for windgalls.' He talked of thoroughpins and sidebones, splints and quittor; things the students wouldn't learn about for another four years, but it brought it all to life.

The words were still spinning in my head as I walked slowly

down the sloping street. This was what I had come for. I felt as though I had undergone an initiation and become a member of an exclusive club. I really knew about horses. And I was wearing a brand new riding mac with all sorts of extra straps and buckles which slapped against my legs as I turned the corner of the hill into busy Newton Road.

I could hardly believe my luck when I saw the horse. It was standing outside the library below Queen's Cross like something left over from another age. It drooped dispiritedly between the shafts of a coal cart which stood like an island in an eddying stream of cars and buses. Pedestrians hurried by, uncaring, but I had the feeling that fortune was smiling on me.

A horse. Not just a picture but a real, genuine horse. Stray words from the lecture floated up into my mind; the pastern, cannon bone, coronet and all those markings – snip, blaze, white sock near hind. I stood on the pavement and examined the animal critically.

I thought it must be obvious to every passer-by that here was a true expert. Not just an inquisitive onlooker but a man who knew and understood all. I felt clothed in a visible aura of horsiness.

I took a few steps up and down, hands deep in the pockets of the new riding mac, eyes probing for possible shoeing faults or curbs or bog spavins. So thorough was my inspection that I worked round to the off side of the horse and stood perilously among the racing traffic.

I glanced around at the people hurrying past. Nobody seemed to care, not even the horse. He was a large one, at least seventeen hands, and he gazed apathetically down the street, easing his hind legs alternatively in a bored manner. I hated to leave him but I had completed my examination and it was time I was on my way. But I felt that I ought to make a gesture before I left; something to communicate to the horse that I understood his problems and that we belonged to the same brotherhood. I stepped briskly forward and patted him on the neck.

Quick as a striking snake, the horse whipped downwards and

seized my shoulder in his great strong teeth. He laid back his ears, rolled his eyes wickedly and hoisted me up, almost off my feet. I hung there helplessly, suspended like a lopsided puppet. I wriggled and kicked but the teeth were clamped immovably in the material of my coat.

There was no doubt about the interest of the passers by now. The grotesque sight of a man hanging from a horse's mouth brought them to a sudden halt and a crowd formed with people looking over each other's shoulders and others fighting at the back to see what was going on.

A horrified old lady was crying: 'Oh, poor boy! Help him, somebody!' Some of the braver characters tried pulling at me but the horse whickered ominously and hung on tighter. Conflicting advice was shouted from all sides. With deep shame I saw two attractive girls in the front row giggling helplessly.

Appalled at the absurdity of my position, I began to thrash about wildly; my shirt collar tightened round my throat; a stream of the horse's saliva trickled down the front of my mac. I could feel myself choking and was giving up hope when a man pushed his way through the crowd.

He was very small. Angry eyes glared from a face blackened by coal dust. Two empty sacks were draped over an arm.

'Whit the hell's this?' he shouted. A dozen replies babbled in the air.

'Can ye no leave the bloody hoarse alone?' he yelled into my face. I made no reply, being pop-eyed, half throttled and in no mood for conversation.

The coalman turned his fury on the horse. 'Drop him, ya big bastard! Go on, let go, drop him!'

Getting no response he dug the animal viciously in the belly with his thumb. The horse took the point at once and released me like an obedient dog dropping a bone. I fell on my knees and ruminated in the gutter for a while till I could breath more easily. As from a great distance I could still hear the little man shouting at me.

After some time I stood up. The coalman was still shouting

and the crowd was listening appreciatively. 'Whit d'ye think you're playing at – keep yer hands off ma bloody hoarse – get the poliss tae ye.'

I looked down at my new mac. The shoulder was chewed to a sodden mass. I felt I must escape and began to edge my way through the crowd. Some of the faces were concerned but most were grinning. Once clear I started to walk away rapidly and as I turned the corner the last faint cry from the coalman reached me.

'Dinna meddle wi' things ye ken nuthin' aboot!'

CHAPTER NINETEEN

I flipped idly through the morning mail. The usual stack of bills, circulars, brightly coloured advertisements for new drugs; after a few months the novelty had worn off and I hardly bothered to read them. I had almost reached the bottom of the pile when I came on something different; an expensive looking envelope in heavy, deckle-edged paper addressed to me personally. I ripped it open and pulled out a gilt coloured card which I scanned quickly. I felt my face redden as I slipped the card into an inside pocket.

Siegfried finished ticking off the visits and looked up. 'What are you looking so guilty about, James? Your past catching up with you. What is it, anyway – a letter from an outraged mother?'

'Go on then,' I said sheepishly, pulling out the card and handing it to him, 'have a good laugh. I suppose you'd find out, anyway.'

Siegfried's face was expressionless as he read the card aloud. 'Tricki requests the pleasure of Uncle Herriot's company on Friday February 5th. Drinks and dancing.' He looked up and spoke seriously. 'Now isn't that nice. You know, that must be one of the most generous Pekingeses in England. Sending you

120

kippers and tomatoes and hampers isn't enough – he has to ask you to his home for a party.'

I grabbed the card and slipped it out of sight. 'All right, all right, I know. But what am I supposed to do?'

'Do? What you do is to sit down right away and get a letter off saying thank you very much, you'll be there on February the fifth. Mrs Pumphrey's parties are famous. Mountains of exotic food, rivers of champagne. Don't miss it whatever you do.'

'Will there be a lot of people there?' I asked, shuffling my feet.

Siegfried struck himself on the forehead with his open hand. 'Of course there'll be a lot of people. What d'you think. Did you expect it would be just you and Tricki? You'd have a few beers together and then you'd dance a slow foxtrot with him? The cream of the county will be there in full regalia but my guess is that there will be no more honoured guest than Uncle Herriot. Why? Because Mrs Pumphrey invited the others but Tricki invited you.'

'OK, OK,' I groaned. 'I'll be on my own and I haven't got a proper evening suit. I don't fancy it.'

Siegfried rose and put a hand on my shoulder. 'My dear chap, don't mess about. Sit down and accept the invitation and then go into Brawton and hire a suit for the night. You won't be on your own for long – the debs will be tramping over each other for a dance with you.' He gave the shoulder a final pat before walking to the door. Before leaving he turned round and his expression was grave. 'And remember for Pete's sake don't write to Mrs Pumphrey. Address your letter to Tricki himself or you're sunk.'

I had a lot of mixed feelings churning around in me when I presented myself at the Pumphrey home on the night of February 5th. A maid let me into the hall and I could see Mrs Pumphrey at the entrance to the ballroom receiving her guests and beyond, an elegant throng standing around with drinks. There was a well bred clamour, a general atmosphere of wealth. I straightened the tie on my hired outfit, took a deep breath and waited.

Mrs Pumphrey was smiling sweetly as she shook hands with the couple in front of me but when she saw me her face became radiant. 'Oh Mr Herriot, how nice of you to come. Tricki was so delighted to have your letter – in fact we really must go in and see him now.' She led me across the hall.

'He's in the morning-room,' she whispered. 'Between ourselves he finds these affairs rather a bore, but he'll be simply furious if I don't take you in for a moment.'

Tricki was curled up in an armchair by the side of a bright fire. When he saw me he jumped on the back of the chair barking in delight, his huge, laughing mouth bisecting his face. I was trying to fend off his attempts to lick my face when I caught sight of two large food bowls on the carpet. One contained about a pound of chopped chicken, the other a mass of crumbled cake.

'Mrs Pumphrey!' I thundered, pointing at the bowls. The poor woman put her hand to her mouth and shrank away from me.

'Oh do forgive me,' she wailed, her face a picture of guilt. 'It's just a special treat because he's alone tonight. And the weather is so cold, too.' She clasped her hands and looked at me abjectly.

'I'll forgive you,' I said sternly, 'If you will remove half the chicken and all the cake.'

Fluttering, like a little girl caught in naughtiness, she did as I said.

I parted regretfully from the little Peke. It had been a busy day and I was sleepy from the hours in the biting cold. The room with its fire and soft lighting looked more inviting than the noisy glitter of the ballroom and I would have preferred to curl up here with Tricki on my knee for an hour or two.

Mrs Pumphrey became brisk. 'Now you must come and meet some of my friends.' We went into the ballroom where light blazed down from three cut glass chandeliers and was reflected dazzlingly from the cream and gold, many-mirrored walls. We moved from group to group as Mrs Pumphrey introduced me and I squirmed in embarrassment as I heard myself described as 'Tricki's dear kind uncle'. But either they were people of superb self control or they were familiar with their hostess's blind spot because the information was received with complete gravity.

Along one wall a five piece orchestra was tuning up; white-jacketed waiters hurried among the guests with trays of food and drinks. Mrs Pumphrey stopped one of the waiters. 'François, some champagne for this gentleman.'

'Yes, Madame.' The waiter proffered his tray.

'No, no, no, not those. One of the big glasses.'

François hurried away and returned with something like a soup plate with a stem. It was brimming with champagne.

'François.'

'Yes, Madame?'

'This is Mr Herriot. I want you to take a good look at him.'

The waiter turned a pair of sad, spaniel eyes on me and drank me in for a few moments.

'I want you to look after him. See that his glass is full and that he has plenty to eat.'

'Certainly, Madame.' He bowed and moved away.

I buried my face in the ice cold champagne and when I looked up, there was François holding out a tray of smoked salmon sandwiches.

It was like that all the evening. François seemed always to be at my elbow, filling up the enormous glass or pushing dainties at me. I found it delightful; the salty snacks brought on a thirst which I quenched with deep draughts of champagne, then I had more snacks which made me thirsty again and François would unfailingly pop up with the magnum.

It was the first time I had had the opportunity of drinking champagne by the pint and it was a rewarding experience. I was quickly aware of a glorious lightness, a heightening of the perceptions. I stopped being overawed by this new world and began to enjoy it. I danced with everybody in sight – sleek young beauties, elderly dowagers and twice with a giggling Mrs Pumphrey.

Or I just talked. And it was witty talk; I repeatedly amazed myself by my lightning shafts. Once I caught sight of myself in the mirror – a distinguished figure, glass in hand, the hired suit hanging on me with quiet grace. It took my breath away.

Eating, drinking, talking, dancing, the evening winged past. When it was time to go and I had my coat on and was shaking hands with Mrs Pumphrey in the hall, François appeared again with a bowl of hot soup. He seemed to be worried lest I grow faint on the journey home.

After the soup, Mrs Pumphrey said: 'And now you must come and say goodnight to Tricki. He'll never forgive you if you don't.' We went into his room and the little dog yawned from the depths of the chair and wagged his tail. Mrs Pumphrey put her hand on my sleeve. 'While you're here, I wonder if you would be so kind as to examine his claws. I've been so worried in case they might be growing too long.'

I lifted up the paws one by one and scrutinized the claws while Tricki lazily licked my hands. 'No, you needn't worry, they're perfectly all right.'

'Thank you so much, I'm so grateful to you. Now you must wash your hands.'

In the familiar bathroom with the sea green basins and the enamelled fishes on the walls and the dressing-table and the bottles on the glass shelves, I looked around as the steaming water ran from the tap. There was my own towel by the basin and the usual new slab of soap – soap that lathered in an instant and gave off an expensive scent. It was the final touch of balm on a gracious evening. It had been a few hours of luxury and light and I carried the memory back with me to Skeldale House.

I got into bed, switched off the light and lay on my back looking up into the darkness. Snatches of music still tinkled about in my head and I was beginning to swim back to the ballroom when the phone rang.

'This is Atkinson of Beck Cottage,' a far away voice said. 'I 'ave a sow 'ere what can't get pigged. She's been on all night. Will you come?'

I looked at the clock as I put down the receiver. It was two AM. I felt numbed. A farrowing right on top of the champagne and the smoked salmon and those little biscuits with the black heaps of caviare. And at Beck Cottage, one of the most primitive smallholdings in the district. It wasn't fair.

Sleepily, I took off my pyjamas and pulled on my shirt. As I reached for the stiff, worn corduroys I used for work, I tried not to look at the hired suit hanging on a corner of the wardrobe.

I groped my way down the long garden to the garage. In the darkness of the yard I closed my eyes and the great chandeliers blazed again, the mirrors flashed and the music played.

It was only two miles out to Beck Cottage. It lay in a hollow and in the winter the place was a sea of mud. I left my car and squelched through the blackness to the door of the house. My knock was unanswered and I moved across to the cluster of buildings opposite and opened the half door into the byre. The warm, sweet bovine smell met me as I peered towards a light showing dimly at the far end where a figure was standing.

I went inside past the shadowy row of cows standing side by side with broken wooden partitions between them and past the mounds of manure piled behind them. Mr Atkinson didn't believe in mucking out too often.

Stumbling over the broken floor, splashing through pools of urine, I arrived at the end where a pen had been made by closing off a corner with a gate. I could just make out the form of a pig, pale in the gloom, lying on her side. There was a scanty bed of straw under her and she lay very still except for the trembling of her flanks. As I watched, she caught her breath and strained for a few seconds then the straining began again.

125

Mr Atkinson received me without enthusiasm. He was middle-aged, sported a week's growth of beard and wore an ancient hat with a brim which flopped round his ears. He stood hunched against a wall, one hand deep in a ragged pocket, the other holding a bicycle lamp with a fast-failing battery.

'Is this all the light we've got?' I asked.

'Aye, it is,' Mr Atkinson replied, obviously surprised. He looked from the lamp to me with a 'what more does he want?' expression.

'Let's have it, then.' I trained the feeble beam on my patient. 'Just a young pig, isn't she?'

'Aye, nobbut a gilt. Fust litter.'

The pig strained again, shuddered and lay still.

'Something stuck there, I reckon,' I said. 'Will you bring me a bucket of hot water some soap and a towel, please.'

'Haven't got no 'ot water. Fire's out.'

'OK, bring me whatever you've got.'

The farmer clattered away down the byre taking the light with him and, with the darkness, the music came back again. It was a Strauss waltz and I was dancing with Lady Frenswick; she was young and very fair and she laughed as I swung her round. I could see her white shoulders and the diamonds winking at her throat and the wheeling mirrors.

Mr Atkinson came shuffling back and dumped a bucket of water on the floor. I dipped a finger in the water; it was ice cold. And the bucket had seen many hard years – I would have to watch my arms on that jagged rim.

Quickly stripping off jacket and shirt, I sucked in my breath as a villainous draught blew through a crack on to my back.

'Soap, please,' I said through clenched teeth.

'In t'bucket.'

I plunged an arm into the water, shivered, and felt my way round till I found a roundish object about the size of a golf ball. I pulled it out and examined it; it was hard and smooth and speckled like a pebble from the sea shore and, optimistically, I began to rub it between my hands and up my arms, waiting for the lather to form. But the soap was impervious; it yielded nothing.

I discarded the idea of asking for another piece in case this would be construed as another complaint. Instead, I borrowed the light and tracked down the byre into the yard, the mud sucking at my Wellingtons, goose pimples rearing on my chest. I searched around in the car boot, listening to my teeth chattering, till I came on a jar of antiseptic lubricating cream.

Back in the pen, I smeared the cream on my arm, knelt behind the pig and gently inserted my hand into the vagina. I moved my hand forward and as wrist and elbow disappeared inside the pig I was forced to roll over on my side. The stones were cold and wet but I forgot my discomfort when my fingers touched something; it was a tiny tail. Almost a transverse presentation, biggish piglet stuck like a cork in a bottle.

Using one finger, I worked the hind legs back until I was able to grasp them and draw the piglet out. 'This is the one that's been causing the trouble. He's dead, I'm afraid – been squashed in there too long. But there could be some live ones still inside. I'll have another feel.'

I greased my arm and got down again. Just inside the os uteri, almost at arm's length, I found another piglet and I was feeling at the face when a set of minute but very sharp teeth sank into my finger.

I yelped and looked up at the farmer from my stony bed. 'This one's alive, anyway. I'll soon have him out.'

But the piglet had other ideas. He showed no desire to leave his warm haven and every time I got hold of his slippery little foot between my fingers he jerked it away. After a minute or two of this game I felt a cramping in my arm. I relaxed and lay back, my head resting on the cobbles, my arm still inside the pig. I closed my eyes and immediately I was back in the ballroom, in the warmth and the brilliant light. I was holding out my immense glass while François poured from the magnum; then I was dancing, close to the orchestra this time and the leader, beating time with one hand, turned round and smiled into my face; smiled and bowed as though he had been looking for me all his life.

I smiled back but the bandleader's face dissolved and there was only Mr Atkinson looking down at me expressionlessly, his unshaven jaw and shaggy eyebrows thrown into sinister relief by the light striking up from the bicycle lamp.

I shook myself and raised my cheek from the floor. This wouldn't do. Falling asleep on the job; either I was very tired or there was still some champagne in me. I reached again and grasped the foot firmly between two fingers and this time, despite his struggles, the piglet was hauled out into the world. Once arrived, he seemed to accept the situation and tottered round philosophically to his mother's udder.

'She's not helping at all,' I said. 'Been on so long that's she's exhausted. I'm going to give her an injection.'

Another numbing expedition through the mud to the car, a shot of pituitrin into the gilt's thigh and within minutes the action began with powerful contractions of the uterus. There was no obstruction now and soon a wriggling pink piglet was deposited in the straw; then quite quickly another and another.

'Coming off the assembly line now, all right,' I said. Mr Atkinson grunted.

Eight piglets had been born and the light from the lamp had almost given out when a dark mass of afterbirth welled from the gilt's vulva..

I rubbed my cold arms. 'Well, I should say that's the lot now.' I felt suddenly chilled; I couldn't say how long I had been standing there looking at the wonder that never grew stale; the little pigs struggling on to their legs and making their way unguided to the long double row of teats; the mother with her first family easing herself over to expose as much as possible of her udder to the hungry mouths.

Better get dressed quickly. I had another try at the marble-like soap but it defeated me as easily as the first time. I wondered how long it had been in the family. Down my right side my cheek and ribs were caked with dirt and mucus. I did my best to scrape some off with my finger nails then I swilled myself down with the cold water from the bucket.

'Have you a towel there?' I gasped.

Mr Atkinson wordlessly handed me a sack. Its edges were stiff with old manure and it smelled musty from the meal it had long since contained. I took it and began to rub my chest and as the sour grains of the meal powdered my skin, the last bubbles of champagne left me, drifted up through the gaps in the tiles and burst sadly in the darkness beyond.

I dragged my shirt over my gritty back, feeling a sense of coming back to my own world. I buttoned my coat, picked up the syringe and the bottle of pituitrin and climbed out of the pen. I had a last look before I left. The bicycle lamp was shedding its final faint glow and I had to lean over the gate to see the row of little pigs sucking busily, utterly absorbed. The gilt carefully shifted her position and grunted. It was a grunt of deep content.

Yes, I was back and it was all right. I drove through the mud and up the hill where I had to get out to open a gate and the wind, with the cold, clean smell of the frosty grass in it caught at my face. I stood for a while looking across the dark fields, thinking of the night which was ending now. My mind went back to my schooldays and an old gentleman talking to the class about careers. He had said: 'If you decide to become a veterinary surgeon you will never grow rich but you will have a life of endless interest and variety.'

I laughed aloud in the darkness and as I got into the car I was still chuckling. That old chap certainly wasn't kidding. Variety. That was it – variety.

CHAPTER TWENTY

As I checked my list of calls it occurred to me that, this time, Siegfried didn't look so much like a schoolboy as he faced Miss Harbottle. For one thing, he hadn't marched straight in and stood in front of the desk; that was disastrous and he always looked beaten before he started. Instead, he had veered off over the last few yards till he stood with his back to the window. This way she had to turn her head slightly to face him and besides, he had the light at his back.

He thrust his hands into his pockets and leaned back against the window frame. He was wearing his patient look, his eyes were kind and his face was illumined by an almost saintly smile. Miss Harbottle's eyes narrowed.

'I just wanted a word with you, Miss Harbottle. One or two little points I'd like to discuss. First, about your petty cash box. It's a nice box and I think you were quite right to institute it, but I think you would be the first to agree that the main function of a cash box is to have cash in it.' He gave a light laugh. 'Now last night I had a few dogs in the surgery and the owners wanted to pay on the spot. I had no change and went for some to your box – it was quite empty. I had to say I would send them a bill, and that isn't good business, is it Miss Harbottle? It didn't look good, so I really must ask you to keep some cash in your cash box.'

Miss Harbottle's eyes widened incredulously. 'But Mr Farnon, you removed the entire contents to go to the hunt ball at . . .'

Siegfried held up a hand and his smile took on an unearthly quality. 'Please hear me out. There is another very small thing I want to bring to your attention. It is now the tenth day of the month and the accounts have not gone out. Now this is a very undesirable state of affairs and there are several points to consider here.'

'But Mr Farnon . . . I'

'Just one moment, Miss Harbottle, till I explain this to you. It is a known fact that farmers pay their bills more readily if they receive them on the first of the month. And there is another, even more important factor.' The beautiful smile left his face and was replaced by an expression of sorrowing gravity. 'Have you ever stopped to work out just how much interest the practice is losing on all the money lying out there because you are late in sending out the accounts.'

'Mr Farnon . . . I'

'I am almost finished, Miss Harbottle, and, believe me, it grieves me to have to speak like this. But the fact is, I can't afford to lose money in this way.' He spread out his hands in a gesture of charming frankness. 'So if you will just apply yourself to this little matter I'm sure all will be well.'

'But will you tell me how I can possibly send the accounts when you refuse to write up the . . .'

'In conclusion, Miss Harbottle, let me say this. I have been very satisfied with your progress since you joined us, and I am sure that with time you will tighten up on those little points I have just mentioned.' A certain roguishness crept into his smile and he put his head on one side. Miss Harbottle's strong fingers closed tightly round a heavy ebony ruler.

'Efficiency,' he said, crinkling his eyes. 'That's what we must have – efficiency.'

CHAPTER TWENTY-ONE

I dropped the suture needle into the tray and stepped back to survey the finished job. 'Well though I say it myself, that looks rather nice.'

Tristan leaned over the unconscious dog and examined the

neat incision with its row of regular stitches. 'Very pretty indeed, my boy. Couldn't have done better myself.'

The big black labrador lay peacefully on the table, his tongue lolling, his eyes glazed and unseeing. He had been brought in with an ugly growth over his ribs and I had decided that it was a simple lipoma, quite benign and very suitable for surgery. And so it had turned out. The tumour had come away with almost ridiculous ease, round, intact and shining, like a hard boiled egg from its shell. No haemorrhage, no fear of recurrence.

The unsightly swelling had been replaced by this tidy scar which would be invisible in a few weeks. I was pleased.

'We'd better keep him here till he comes round,' I said. 'Give me a hand to get him on to these blankets.' We made the dog comfortable in front of an electric stove and I left to start my morning round.

It was during lunch that we first heard the strange sound. It was something between a moan and a howl, starting quite softly but rising to a piercing pitch before shuddering back down the scale to silence.

Siegfried looked up, startled, from his soup. 'What in God's name is that?'

'Must be that dog I operated on this morning,' I replied. 'The odd one does that coming out of barbiturates. I expect he'll stop soon.'

Siegfried looked at me doubtfully. 'Well, I hope so – I could soon get tired of that. Gives me the creeps.'

We went through and looked at the dog. Pulse strong, respirations deep and regular, mucous membranes a good colour. He was still stretched out, immobile, and the only sign of returning consciousness was the howl which seemed to have settled down into a groove of one every ten seconds.

'Yes, he's perfectly all right,' Siegfried said. 'But what a bloody noise! Let's get out of here.'

Lunch was finished hastily and in silence except for the ceaseless background wailing. Siegfried had scarcely swallowed his last mouthful before he was on his feet. 'Well, I must fly. Got a lot on this afternoon. Tristan, I think it would be a good idea to bring that dog through to the sitting-room and put him by the fire. Then you could stay by him and keep an eye on him.'

Tristan was stunned. 'You mean I have to stay in the same room as that noise all afternoon?'

'Yes, I mean just that. We can't send him home as he is and I don't want anything to happen to him. He needs care and attention.'

'Maybe you'd like me to hold his paw or perhaps wheel him round the market place?'

'Don't give me any of your bloody cheek. You stay with the dog and that's an order!'

Tristan and I stretchered the heavy animal along the passage on the blankets, then I had to leave for the afternoon round. I paused and looked back at the big black form by the fire and Tristan crouched miserably in his chair. The noise was overpowering. I closed the door hurriedly.

It was dark when I got back and the old house hung over me, black and silent against the frosty sky. Silent, that is, except for the howling which still echoed along the passage and filtered eerily into the deserted street.

I glanced at my watch as I slammed the car door. It was six o'clock, so Tristan had had four hours of it. I ran up the steps and along the passage and when I opened the sitting-room door the noise jarred in my head. Tristan was standing with his back to me, looking through the french window into the darkness of the garden. His hands were deep in his pockets; tufts of cotton wool drooped from his ears.

'Well, how is it going?' I asked.

There was no reply so I walked over and tapped him on the shoulder. The effect was spectacular. Tristan leaped into the air and corkscrewed round. His face was ashen and he was trembling violently.

'God help us, Jim, you nearly killed me there. I can't hear a

133

damn thing through these ear plugs – except the dog, of course. Nothing keeps that out.'

I knelt by the labrador and examined him. The dog's condition was excellent but, except for a faint eye reflex there was no sign that he was regaining consciousness. And all the time there were the piercing, evenly spaced howls.

'He's taking a hell of a time to come out of it,' I said. 'Has he been like this all afternoon?'

'Yes, just like that. Not one bit different. And don't waste any sympathy on him, the yowling devil. He's as happy as a sandboy down by the fire – doesn't know a thing about it. But how about me? My nerves are about shot to bits listening to him hour after hour. Much more of it and you'll have to give me a shot too.' He ran a shaking hand through his hair and a twitching started in his cheek.

I took his arm. 'Well, come through and eat. You'll feel better after some food.' I led him unresisting into the dining-room.

Siegfried was in excellent form over the meal. He seemed to be in a mood of exhilaration and monopolized the conversation but he did not once refer to the shrill obligato from the other room. There was no doubt, however, that it was still getting through to Tristan.

As they were leaving the room, Siegfried put his hand on my shoulder. 'Remember we've got that meeting in Brawton tonight, James. Old Reeves on diseases of sheep – he's usually very good. Pity you can't come too, Tristan, but I'm afraid you'll have to stay with the dog till he comes round.'

Tristan flinched as if he had been struck. 'Oh not another session with that bloody animal! He's driving me mad!'

'I'm afraid there's nothing else for it. James or I could have taken over tonight but we have to show up at this meeting. It would look bad if we missed it.'

Tristan stumbled back into the room and I put on my coat. As I went out into the street I paused for a moment and listened. The dog was still howling.

The meeting was a success. It was held in one of Brawton's lush hotels and, as usual, the best part was the get together of the vets in the bar afterwards. It was infinitely soothing to hear the other man's problems and mistakes – especially the mistakes.

It amused me to look round the crowded room and try to guess what the little knots of men were talking about. That man over there, bent double and slashing away at the air with one hand – he was castrating a colt in the standing position. And the one with his arm out at full stretch, his fingers working busily at nothing – almost certainly foaling a mare; probably correcting a carpal flexion. And doing it effortlessly too. Veterinary surgery was a childishly simple matter in a warm bar with a few drinks inside you.

It was eleven o'clock before we all got into our cars and headed for our own particular niche in Yorkshire – some to the big industrial towns of the West Riding, others to the seaside places of the East coast and Siegfried and I hurrying thankfully back on the narrow road which twisted between its stone walls into the Northern Pennines.

I thought guiltily that for the last few hours I had completely forgotten about Tristan and his vigil. Still, it must have been better tonight. The dog would surely have quietened down by now. But, jumping from the car in Darrowby, I froze in mid stride as a thin wail came out faintly from Skeldale House. This was incredible; it was after midnight and the dog was still at it. And what of Tristan? I hated to think what kind of shape he'd be in. Almost fearfully I turned the knob on the sitting-room door.

Tristan's chair made a little island in a sea of empty beer bottles. An upturned crate lay against the wall and Tristan was sitting very upright and looking solemn. I picked my way over the debris.

'Well, has it been rough, Triss? How do you feel now?'

'Could be worse, old lad, could be worse. Soon as you'd gone I slipped over to the Drovers for a crate of pint Magnets. Made all the difference. After three or four the dog stopped worrying me – matter of fact, I've been yowling back at him for hours now. We've had quite an interesting evening. Anyway, he's coming out now. Look at him.'

The big dog had his head up and there was recognition in his eyes. The howling had stopped. I went over and patted him and the long black tail jerked in a fair attempt at a wag.

'That's better, old boy,' I said. 'But you'd better behave yourself now. You've given your uncle Tristan one hell of a day.'

The labrador responded immediately by struggling to his feet. He took a few swaying steps and collapsed among the bottles.

Siegfried appeared in the doorway and looked distastefully at Tristan, still very upright and wearing a judicial expression, and at the dog scrabbling among the bottles. 'What an infernal mess! Surely you can do a little job without making an orgy out of it.'

At the sound of his voice the labrador staggered up and, in a flush of over confidence, tried to run towards him, wagging his tail unsteadily. He didn't get very far and went down in a heap, sending an empty Magnet rolling gently up to Siegfried's feet.

Siegfried bent over and stroked the shining black head. 'Nice friendly animal that. I should think he's a grand dog when he's got his senses about him. He'll be normal in the morning, but the problem is what to do with him now. We can't leave him staggering about down here – he could break a leg.' He glanced at Tristan who had not moved a muscle. He was sitting up straighter than ever; stiff and motionless like a Prussian general. 'You know, I think the best thing would be for you to take him up to your room tonight. Now we've got him so far, we don't want him to hurt himself. Yes, that's it, he can spend the night with you.'

'Thank you, thank you very much indeed,' Tristan said in a flat voice, still looking straight to his front.

Siegfried looked at him narrowly for a moment, then turned away. 'Right then, clear away this rubbish and let's get to bed.'

My bedroom and Tristan's were connected by a door. Mine was the main room, huge, square, with a high ceiling, pillared fireplace and graceful alcoves like the ones downstairs. I always felt a little like a duke lying there.

Tristan's had been the old dressing-room and was long and narrow with his small bed crouching at one end as if trying to hide. There were no carpets on the smooth, varnished boards so I laid the dog on a heap of blankets and talked down soothingly at Tristan's wan face on the pillow.

'He's quiet now – sleeping like a baby and looks as though he's going to stay that way. You'll be able to have a well earned rest now.'

I went back to my own room, undressed quickly and got into bed. I went to sleep immediately and I couldn't tell just when the noises started next door, but I came suddenly wide awake with an angry yell ringing in my ears. Then there was a slithering and a bump followed by another distracted cry from Tristan.

I quailed at the idea of going into the dressing-room – there was nothing I could do, anyway – so I huddled closer into the sheets and listened. I kept sliding into a half sleep then starting into wakefulness at more bumping and shouting came through the wall.

After about two hours the noises began to change. The labrador seemed to have gained mastery over his legs and was marching up and down the room, his claws making a regular tck-a-tck, tck-a-tck, tck-a-tck on the wooden floor. It went on and on, interminably. At intervals, Tristan's voice, hoarse now, burst out. 'Stop it, for Christ's sake! Sit down, you bloody dog!'

I must have fallen into a deeper sleep because when I awoke the room was grey with the cold light of morning. I rolled on to my back and listened. I could still hear the tck-a-tck of the claws but it had become irregular as though the labrador was strolling about instead of blundering blindly from one end of the room to the other. There was no sound from Tristan.

I got out of bed, shivering as the icy air of the room gripped me, and pulled on my shirt and trousers. Tiptoeing across the floor, I opened the connecting door and was almost floored as two large feet were planted on my chest. The labrador was delighted to see me and appeared to be thoroughly at home. His fine brown eyes shone with intelligence and well-being and he showed rows of glittering teeth and a flawlessly pink tongue in a wide, panting grin. Far below, the tail lashed ecstatically.

'Well, you're all right, chum,' I said. 'Let's have a look at that wound.' I removed the horny paws from my chest and explored the line of stitches over the ribs. No swelling, no pain, no reaction at all.

'Lovely!' I cried. 'Beautiful. You're as good as new again.' I gave the dog a playful slap on the rump which sent him into a transport of joy. He leaped all over me, clawing and licking.

I was fighting him off when I heard a dismal groan from the bed. In the dim light Tristan looked ghastly. He was lying on his back, both hands clutching the quilt and there was a wild look in his eyes. 'Not a wink of sleep, Jim,' he whispered. 'Not a bloody wink. He's got a wonderful sense of humour, my brother, making me spend the night with this animal. It'll really make his day when he hears what I've been through. Just watch him — I'll bet you anything you like he'll look pleased.'

Later, over breakfast, Siegfried heard the details of his brother's harrowing night and was very sympathetic. He condoled with him at length and apologized for all the trouble the dog had given him. But Tristan was right. He did look pleased.

CHAPTER TWENTY-TWO

As I came into the operating room I saw that Siegfried had a patient on the table. He was thoughtfully stroking the head of an elderly and rather woebegone border terrier.

'James,' he said, 'I want you to take this little dog through to Grier.'

'Grier?'

'Vet at Brawton. He was treating the case before the owner moved into our district. I've seen it a couple of times — stones in the bladder. It needs an immediate operation and I think I'd better let Grier do it. He's a touchy devil and I don't want to stand on his toes.'

'Oh, I think I've heard of him,' I said.

'Probably you have. A cantankerous Aberdonian. Since he practises in a fashionable town he gets quite a few students and he gives them hell. That sort of thing gets around.' He lifted the terrier from the table and handed him to me. 'The sooner you get through there the better. You can see the op and bring the dog back here afterwards. But watch yourself — don't rub Grier the wrong way or he'll take it out of you somehow.'

At my first sight of Angus Grier I thought immediately of whisky. He was about fifty and something had to be responsible for the fleshy, mottled cheeks, the swimmy eyes and the pattern of purple veins which chased each other over his prominent nose. He wore a permanently insulted expression.

He didn't waste any charm on me; a nod and a grunt and he grabbed the dog from my arms. Then he stabbed a finger at a slight, fairish youth in a white coat. 'That's Clinton — final year student. Do ye no' think there's some pansy lookin' buggers coming in to this profession?'

During the operation he niggled constantly at the young man and, in an attempt to create a diversion, I asked when he was going back to college.

'Beginning of next week,' he replied.

'Aye, but he's awa hame tomorrow,' Grier rasped. 'Wasting his time when he could be gettin' good experience here.'

The student blushed. 'Well, I've been seeing practice for over a month and I felt I ought to spend a couple of days with my mother before the term starts.'

'Oh, I ken, I ken. You're all the same – canna stay away from the titty.'

The operation was uneventful and as Grier inserted the last stitch he looked up at me. 'You'll no' want to take the dog back till he's out of the anaesthetic. I've got a case to visit – you can come with me to pass the time.'

We didn't have what you could call a conversation in the car. It was a monologue; a long recital of wrongs suffered at the hands of wicked clients and predatory colleagues. The story I liked best was about a retired admiral who had asked Grier to examine his horse for soundness. Grier said the animal had a bad heart and was not fit to ride, whereupon the admiral flew into a fury and got another vet to examine the horse. The second vet said there was nothing the matter with the heart and passed the animal sound.

The admiral wrote Grier a letter and told him what he thought of him in fairly ripe quarter-deck language. Having got this out of his system he felt refreshed and went out for a ride during which, in the middle of a full gallop the horse fell down dead and rolled on the admiral who sustained a compound fracture of the leg and a crushed pelvis.

'Man,' said Grier with deep sincerity, 'Man, I was awfu' glad.'

We drew up in a particularly dirty farmyard and Grier turned to me. 'I've got a cow tae cleanse here.'

'Right,' I said, 'fine.' I settled down in my seat and took out

my pipe. Grier paused, halfway out of the car. 'Are you no'
coming to give me a hand?'

I couldn't understand him. 'Cleansing' of cows is simply the
removal of retained afterbirth and is a one man job.

'Well, there isn't much I can do is there?' I said. 'And my
Wellingtons and coat are back in my car. I didn't realize it was
a farm visit – I'd probably get messed up for nothing.'

I knew immediately that I'd said the wrong thing. The toad-
skin jowls flushed darker and he gave me a malevolent glance
before turning away; but halfway across the yard he stopped
and stood for a few moments in thought before coming back
to the car. 'I've just remembered. I've got something here you
can put on. You might as well come in with me – you'll be able
to pass me a pessary when I want one.'

It sounded nutty to me, but I got out of the car and went
round to the back. Grier was fishing out a large wooden box
from his boot.

'Here, ye can put this on. It's a calving outfit I got a bit ago.
I haven't used it much because I found it a mite heavy, but it'll
keep ye grand and clean.'

I looked in the box and saw a suit of thick, black, shining
rubber. I lifted out the jacket; it bristled with zip fasteners
and press studs and felt as heavy as lead. The trousers were
even more weighty, with many clips and fasteners. The whole
thing was a most imposing creation, obviously designed by
somebody who had never seen a cow calved and having the
disadvantage that anybody wearing it would be pretty well
immobilized.

I studied Grier's face for a moment but the watery eyes told
me nothing. I began to take off my jacket – it was crazy but I
didn't want to offend the man.

And, in truth, Grier seemed anxious to get me into the suit
because he was holding it up in a helpful manner. It was a two
man operation. First the gleaming trousers were pulled on and
zipped up fore and aft, then it was the turn of the jacket, a
wonderful piece of work, fitting tightly round the waist and

possessing short sleeves about six inches long with powerful elastic gripping my biceps.

Before I could get it on I had to roll my shirt sleeves to the shoulder, then Grier, heaving and straining, worked me into it. I could hear the zips squeaking into place, the final one being at the back of my neck to close a high, stiff collar which held my head in an attitude of supplication, my chin pointing at the sky.

Grier's heart really seemed to be in his work and, for the final touch, he produced a black rubber skull cap. I shrank away from the thing and began to mouth such objections as the collar would allow, but Grier insisted. 'Stand still a wee minute longer. We might as well do the job right.'

When he had finished he stood back admiringly. I must have been a grotesque sight, sheathed from head to foot in gleaming black, my arms, bare to the shoulders, sticking out almost at right angles. Grier appeared well satisfied. 'Well, come on, it's time we got on wi' the job.' He turned and hurried towards the byre; I plodded ponderously after him like an automaton.

Our arrival in the byre caused a sensation. There were present the farmer, two cowmen and a little girl. The men's cheerful greeting froze on their lips as the menacing figure paced slowly, deliberately in. The little girl burst into tears and ran outside.

'Cleansing' is a dirty, smelly job for the operator and a bore for the onlooker who may have to stand around for twenty minutes without being able to see anything. But this was one time the spectators were not bored. Grier was working away inside the cow and mumbling about the weather, but the men weren't listening; they never took their eyes away from me as I stood rigid, like a suit of armour against the wall. They studied each part of the outfit in turn, wonderingly. I knew what they were thinking. Just what was going to happen when this formidable unknown finally went into action. Anybody dressed like that must have some tremendous task ahead of him.

The intense pressure of the collar against my larynx kept me entirely out of any conversation and this must have added to my air of mystery. I began to sweat inside the suit.

The little girl had plucked up courage and brought her brothers and sisters to look at me. I could see the row of little heads peeping round the door and, screwing my head round painfully, I tried to give them a reassuring smile; but the heads disappeared and I heard their feet clattering across the yard.

I couldn't say how long I stood there, but Grier at last finished his job and called out, 'All right, I'm ready for you now.' The atmosphere became suddenly electric. The men straightened up and stared at me with slightly open mouths. This was the moment they had been waiting for.

I pushed myself away from the wall and did a right turn with some difficulty before heading for the tin of pessaries. It was only a few yards away but it seemed a long way as I approached it like a robot, head in the air, arms extended stiffly on either side. When I arrived at the tin I met a fresh difficulty; I could not bend. After a few contortions I got my hand into the tin, then had to take the paper off the pessary with one hand; a new purgatory. The men watched in fascinated silence.

Having removed the paper, I did a careful about turn and paced back along the byre with measured tread. When I came level with the cow I extended my arm stiffly to Grier who took the pessary and inserted it in the uterus.

I then took up my old position against the wall while my colleague cleaned himself down. I glanced down my nose at the men; their expressions had changed to open disbelief. Surely the mystery man's assignment was tougher than that – he couldn't be wearing that outfit just to hand over a pessary. But when Grier started the complicated business of snapping open the studs and sliding the zips they realized the show was over; and fast on the feeling of let-down came amusement.

As I tried to rub some life back into my swollen arms which had been strangulated by the elastic sleeves, I was surrounded by grinning faces. They could hardly wait, I imagined, to get round to the local that night to tell the tale. Pulling together the shreds of my dignity, I put on my jacket and got into the car. Grier stayed to say a few words to the men, but he wasn't holding their attention; it was all on me, huddling in the seat. They couldn't believe I was true.

Back at the surgery the border terrier was coming out of the anaesthetic. He raised his head and tried bravely to wag his tail when he saw me. I wrapped him in a blanket, gathered him up and was preparing to leave when I saw Grier through the partly open door of a small store room. He had the wooden box on a table and he was lifting out the rubber suit, but there was something peculiar about the way he was doing it; the man seemed to be afflicted by a kind of rigor – his body shook and jerked, the mottled face was strangely contorted and a half stifled wailing issued from his lips.

I stared in amazement. I would have said it was impossible, yet it was happening right in front of me. There was not a shadow of a doubt about it – Angus Grier was laughing.

CHAPTER TWENTY-THREE

Milk fever is one of the straightforward conditions, but, looking down into the beck in the dreary dawn light, I realized that this was one of its more bizarre manifestations. The illness had struck immediately after calving and the cow had slithered down the muddy bank into the water. She was unconscious when I arrived, her hindquarters completely submerged, the head resting on a shelf of rock. Her calf, sodden and pathetic in the driving rain, trembled by her side.

Dan Cooper's eyes were anxious as we made our way down. 'I doubt we're too late. She's dead, isn't she? I can't see her breathing.'

'Pretty far gone, I'm afraid,' I replied, 'but I think there's

144

still life there. If I can get some calcium into her vein she might still come round.'

'Damn, I 'ope so,' Dan grunted. 'She's one of my best milkers. It allus happens to the good 'uns.'

'It does with milk fever, anyway. Here, hold these bottles for me.' I pulled out the syringe box and selected a wide-bored needle. My fingers, numb with the special kind of cold you felt in the early morning with your circulation sluggish and your stomach empty, could hardly hold it. The water was deeper than I thought and it was over my Wellington tops at the first stride. Gasping, I bent down and dug my thumb into the jugular furrow at the base of the neck. The vein came up and as I pushed the needle in, the blood ran warm and dark over my hand. I fumbled the flutter valve from my pocket, pushed a bottle into the cup end and inserted the other end into the needle. The calcium began to flow into the vein.

Standing there in the icy beck, holding the bottle aloft with bloody fingers and feeling the rain working its way inside my collar, I tried to keep out the black thoughts; about all those people I knew who were still in bed and would only leave it when their alarm clocks rang; and they would read their papers over breakfast and drive out to their cosy banks or insurance offices. Maybe I should have been a doctor – they treated their patients in nice, warm bedrooms.

I pulled the needle from the vein and threw the empty bottle on to the bank. There was no response to the injection. I took the other bottle and began to run more calcium under the skin. Might as well go through the motions, futile though it seemed now. It was when I was rubbing away the subcutaneous injection that I noticed the eyelids quiver.

A quick ripple of relief and excitement went through me. I looked up at the farmer and laughed. 'She's still with us, Dan.' I flicked her ear and her eyes opened wide. 'We'll wait a few minutes and then try to roll her on to her chest.'

Within a quarter of an hour she was beginning to toss her head about and I knew it was time. I caught hold of her horns and pulled while Dan and his tall son pushed at her shoulder. We made slow progress but after several concerted heaves the cow took over herself and settled on her chest. Immediately everything looked rosier; when a cow is lying on her side she always has the look of death on her.

I was pretty sure then that she would recover, but I couldn't go away and leave her lying in the beck. Milk fever cows can stay down for days on end but I had the feeling this one would be up soon. I decided to stick it out a bit longer.

She didn't seem to relish her situation in the peaty water and began to make determined efforts to rise, but it was another half hour and my teeth were chattering uncontrollably before she finally staggered to her feet.

'Well, that's a licker!' Dan said. 'Ah never thought she'd stand again. Must be good stuff you gave her.'

'It's a bit quicker than the old bicycle pump,' I laughed. The spectacular effects of intravenous calcium were still enough of a novelty to intrigue me. For generations, cows with milk fever had just died. Then inflation of the udder had saved many; but the calcium was the thing – when they got up within an hour like this one, I always felt like a successful conjurer.

We guided the cow up the bank and at the top, the full force of the wind and rain struck us. The house was only a hundred yards away and we battled towards it, Dan and his son leading, holding the calf in a sack slung between them. The tiny animal swung to and fro, screwing up its eyes against the hard world it had entered. Close behind followed the anxious mother, still rocky on her legs but doing her best to poke her muzzle into the sack. I squelched along in the rear.

We left the cow knee deep in straw in a warm shed, licking her calf vigorously. In the porch of the house, the others dutifully pulled off their Wellingtons; I did the same, pouring about a pint of beck water from each boot. Mrs Cooper had the reputation of being a firebrand who exercised an iron rule over Dan and her family, but from my previous contacts with her I had the feeling that Dan didn't do so badly.

I thought so again as I saw her, square built but comely, plaiting a little girl's pigtails in readiness for school. A crackling fire was mirrored in the gleaming brass of the hearth and above the clean farmhouse smell there was a hint of home-cured bacon just beginning to fry.

Mrs Cooper sent Dan and the boy scurrying upstairs to change their socks then she turned a calm gaze on me as I dripped on her linoleum. She shook her head as though I were a naughty child.

'All right, off with the socks,' she rapped out. 'And your coat, and roll up your trousers, and sit down here, and dry your hair with this.' A clean towel landed on my lap and Mrs Cooper bent over me. 'Don't you ever think of wearing a hat?'

'Not keen on them, I'm afraid,' I mumbled, and she shook her head again.

She poured hot water from a kettle into a large bowl and added mustard from a pound tin. 'Here, stick your feet in this.'

I had obeyed all her commands with alacrity and I gave an involuntary yelp as I made contact with the bubbling mixture. At this, she shot a fierce glance at me and I took care to keep my feet in the bowl. I was sitting, teeth clenched, enveloped in steam, when she pushed a pint pot of tea into my hand.

It was old fashioned treatment but effective. By the time I was halfway down the pint pot I felt as though I were being consumed by fire. The river bed chill was a dream which vanished completely as Mrs Cooper topped up my bowl with another scalding quart from the kettle.

Next, she grabbed chair and bowl and swivelled me round till I was sitting at the table, still with my feet in the water. Dan and the children were already at their breakfast and in front of me was a plate with two eggs, a rough cut piece of bacon and several sausages. I had learned enough of Dales ways to keep quiet at meals; when I first came to the district I had thought it incumbent on me to provide light conversation in return for their hospitality but the questioning glances they exchanged with each other silenced me effectively.

So this morning, I attacked the food without preamble, but the first mouthful almost made me break my new found rule. It was the first time I had tasted a home made Yorkshire sausage and it was an effort to restrain the cries of congratulation which would have been natural in other circles. But Mrs Cooper had been watching me out of the corner of her eye and she must have noticed my rapt expression. Casually, she rose, brought over the frying pan and rolled a few more links on to my plate.

'Killed a pig last week,' she said, pulling open the pantry door. I could see the dishes heaped with chopped meat, spare rib, liver, the rows of pies with the jelly gleaming on their pale gold crusts.

I finished my meal, pulled on a thick pair of socks borrowed from Dan and my dry shoes. I was about to leave when Mrs Cooper tucked a parcel under my arm. I knew it contained further samples from the pantry but her eyes dared me to say much about it. I muttered a few words of thanks and went out to the car.

The church clock was chiming a quarter past nine when I pulled up outside Skeldale House. I felt good – warm, full of superb food and with the satisfying memory of the cow's quick recovery. And there was my parcel on the back seat; it was always a stroke of luck to land on a farm after a pig killing and there was usually a gift from the hospitable farmers, but these sausages were something I would never forget.

I took the surgery steps at a jump and trotted along the passage, but as I rounded the corner my progress was halted. Siegfried was standing there, rigid, his back pressed against the wall. Over his shoulder dangled a long, flexible, leather probang. Between us was the half open door of the office with Miss Harbottle clearly visible at her desk.

I waved cheerfully. 'Hello, hello, off to a choke?'

Siegfried's face twisted in anguish and he held up a warning hand. Then he began to creep past the door, balancing on the balls of his feet like a tightrope walker. He was beyond the door and the tense lines of his body had begun to relax when the brass end of the swinging probang clattered against the wall and, as if in reply came the familiar rumble from Miss Harbottle's corner. Siegfried gave me a single despairing glance then, shoulders drooping, he went slowly into the room.

Watching him go, I thought wonderingly of how things had built up since the secretary's arrival. It was naked war now and it gave life an added interest to observe the tactics of the two sides.

At the beginning it seemed that Siegfried must run out an easy winner. He was the employer; he held the reins and it appeared that Miss Harbottle would be helpless in the face of his obstructive strategy. But Miss Harbottle was a fighter and a resourceful one and it was impossible not to admire the way she made use of the weapons at her command.

In fact, over the past week the tide had been running in her favour. She had been playing Siegfried like an expert fisherman with a salmon; bringing him repeatedly back to her desk to answer footling questions. Her throat clearing had developed into an angry bark which could penetrate the full extent of the house. And she had a new weapon; she had taken to writing Siegfried's clerical idiocies on slips of paper; mis-spellings, errors in addition, wrong entries – they were all faithfully copied down.

Miss Harbottle used these slips as ammunition. She never brought one out when things were slack and her employer was hanging about the surgery. She saved them until he was under pressure, then she would push a slip under his nose and say 'How about this?'

She always kept an expressionless face at these times and it was impossible to say how much pleasure it gave her to see him cower back like a whipped animal. But the end was un-varying – mumbled explanations and apologies from Siegfried and Miss Harbottle, radiating self-righteousness, correcting the entry.

As Siegfried went into the room I watched through the partly open door. I knew my morning round was waiting but I was impelled by morbid curiosity. Miss Harbottle, looking brisk and businesslike, was tapping an entry in the book with her pen while Siegfried shuffled his feet and muttered replies. He made several vain attempts to escape and, as the time passed, I could see he was nearing breaking point. His teeth were clenched and his eyes had started to bulge.

The phone rang and the secretary answered it. Her employer was making again for the door when she called happily, 'Colonel Brent for you.' Like a man in a dream he turned back. The Colonel, a racehorse owner, had been a thorn in our flesh for a long time with his complaints and his continual questioning and probing; a call from him was always liable to send up the blood pressure.

I could see it was that way this morning. The minutes ticked away and Siegfried's face got redder. He made his replies in a choked voice which finally rose almost to a shout. At the end he crashed the receiver down and leaned on the desk, breathing heavily.

Then, as I watched, unbelieving, Miss Harbottle began to open the drawer where she kept her slips. She fished one out, coughed and held it in Siegfried's face.

'How about this?' she asked.

I resisted the impulse to close my eyes and stared in horror. For a few seconds nothing happened and there was a tense interval while Siegfried stood quite motionless. Then his face seemed to break up and with a scything sweep of his arm he snatched the slip from the secretary's hand and began to tear at it with fierce intensity. He didn't say a word but as he tore, he leaned forward over the desk and his glaring eyes approached ever nearer to Miss Harbottle who slowly edged her chair back till it was jammed against the wall.

It was a weird picture. Miss Harbottle straining back, her mouth slightly open, her tinted curls bobbing in alarm, and Siegfried, his ravaged features close to hers, still tearing with insane vigour at the piece of paper. The scene ended when

Siegfried, putting every ounce of his strength into an action like a javelin thrower, hurled the torn up slip at the waste paper basket. It fell in a gentle shower, like confetti, in and around the basket and Siegfried, still without speaking, wrapped his probang around him and strode from the room.

In the kitchen, Mrs Hall opened the parcel and extracted a pie, a chunk of liver and a cluster of the exquisite sausages. She turned a quizzical eye on me. 'You look kind of pleased with yourself this morning, Mr Herriot.'

I leaned back against the oak dresser. 'Yes, Mrs Hall, I've just been thinking. It must be very nice to be the principal of a practice but, you know, it's not such a bad life being an assistant.'

CHAPTER TWENTY-FOUR

The day had started badly. Tristan had been trapped by his brother at 4 AM returning from the Bellringers' Outing.

This function took place annually when a bus load of the bellringers of all the local churches made a trip to Morecambe. They spent very little time on the beach, however, and when they weren't working their way from one pub to another, they were attacking the crates of beer they had brought with them.

When they rolled into Darrowby in the small hours most of the occupants of the bus were unconscious. Tristan, an honoured guest of the party, had been tipped out in the back lane behind Skeldale House. He waved weakly as the bus moved away, but drew no response from the unseeing faces at the windows. Lurching down the garden path, he was horrified to see a light in Siegfried's room. Escape was impossible and, when asked to explain where he had been, he made a series of attempts to articulate 'Bellringers' Outing' without success.

Siegfried, seeing he was wasting his time, had saved his

wrath till breakfast time. That was when Tristan told me the story – just before his brother came into the dining-room and started on him.

But, as usual, it seemed to take more out of Siegfried who went off on his rounds glowering and hoarse from shouting. Ten minutes after he had gone I found Tristan closeted cheerfully in Boardman's cubby hole, Boardman listening to some fresh material from the backs of the envelopes and sniggering appreciatively.

The old man had cheered up greatly since Tristan came home and the two of them spent a lot of time in the gloom where the light from the tiny window picked out the rows of rusting tools, the Bairnsfather cartoons looking down from the wall. The place was usually kept locked and visitors were not encouraged; but Tristan was always welcome.

Often, when I was passing by, I would peep in and see Tristan patiently pulling at a Woodbine while Boardman rambled on. 'We was six weeks up the line. The French was on our right and the Jocks on our left . . .' or 'Poor old Fred – one minute 'e was standing by me and next 'e was gone. Never found as much as a trouser button . . .'

This morning, Tristan hailed me boisterously and I marvelled again at his resilience and his power to bend like a willow before the winds of misfortune and spring back unscathed. He held up two tickets.

'Village dance tonight, Jim, and I can guarantee it. Some of my harem from the hospital are going, so I'll see you're all right. And that's not all – look here.' He went into the saddle room, lifted out a loose board and produced a bottle of sherry. 'We'll be able to have a toothful between dances.'

I didn't ask where the tickets or the sherry had come from. I liked the village dances. The packed hall with the three piece band at one end – piano, scraping fiddle and drums – and at the other end, the older ladies looking after the refreshments. Glasses of milk, mounds of sandwiches, ham, home-made brawn, trifles heaped high with cream.

That evening, Tristan came out with me on my last visit and in the car the talk was all about the dance. The case was simple enough – a cow with an infected eye – but the farm was in a village high up the dale, and when we finished, it was dusk. I felt good, and everything seemed to stand out, clear and meaningful. The single, empty, grey stone street, the last red streaks in the sky, the dark purple of the enclosing fells. There was no wind, but a soft breath came from the quiet moors, sweet and fresh and full of promise. Among the houses, the thrilling smell of wood smoke was everywhere.

When we got back to the surgery, Siegfried was out but there was a note for Tristan propped up on the mantelpiece. It said simply: 'Tristan. Go home. Siegfried.'

This had happened before, everything in Skeldale House being in short supply, especially beds and blankets. When unexpected visitors arrived, Tristan was packed off to stay with his mother in Brawton. Normally he would board a train without comment, but tonight was different.

'Good God,' he said. 'Somebody must be coming for the night and, of course, I'm the one who's just expected to disappear. It's a nice bloody carry on, I must say! And isn't that a charming letter! It doesn't matter if I've made any private arrangements. Oh no! There's no question of asking me if it's convenient to leave. It's just "Tristan, go home." Polite and thoughtful, isn't it?'

It was unusual for him to get worked up like this. I spoke soothingly. 'Look, Triss. Maybe we'd better just skip this dance. There'll be others.'

Tristan clenched his fists. 'Why should I let him push me around like this?' he fumed. 'I'm a person, am I not? I have my own life to lead and I tell you I am not going to Brawton tonight. I've arranged to go to a dance and I am damn well going to a dance.'

This was fighting talk but I felt a twinge of alarm. 'Wait a minute. What about Siegfried? What's he going to say when he comes in and finds you still here?'

'To hell with Siegfried!' said Tristan. So I left it at that.

Siegfried came home when we were upstairs, changing. I was first down and found him sitting by the fire, reading. I said nothing but sat down and waited for the explosion.

After a few minutes, Tristan came in. He had chosen with care among his limited wardrobe and was resplendent in a dark grey suit; a scrubbed face shone under carefully combed hair; he was wearing a clean collar.

Siegfried flushed as he looked up from his book. 'What the bloody hell are you doing here? I told you to go to Brawton. Joe Ramage is coming tonight.'

'Couldn't go.'

'Why not?'

'No trains.'

'What the hell do you mean, no trains?'

'Just that – no trains.'

The cross talk was bringing on the usual sense of strain in me. The interview was falling into the habitual pattern; Siegfried red faced, exasperated; his brother expressionless, answering in a flat monotone, fighting a defensive battle with the skill of long practice.

Siegfried sank back in his chair, baffled for the moment, but he kept a slit-eyed gaze on his brother. The smart suit, the slicked hair and polished shoes all seemed to irritate him further.

'All right,' he said suddenly, 'it's maybe just as well you are staying. I want you to do a job for me. You can open that haematoma on Charlie Dent's pig's ear.'

This was a bombshell. Charlie Dent's pig's ear was something we didn't talk about.

A few weeks earlier, Siegfried himself had gone to the small-holding halfway along a street on the outskirts of the town to see a pig with a swollen ear. It was an aural haematoma and the only treatment was to lance it, but for some reason, Siegfried had not done the job but had sent me the following day.

I had wondered about it, but not for long. When I climbed into the sty, the biggest sow I had ever seen rose from the straw, gave an explosive bark and rushed at me with its huge mouth gaping. I didn't stop to argue. I made the wall about six inches ahead of the pig and vaulted over into the passage. I stood there, considering the position, looking thoughtfully at the mean little red eyes, the slavering mouth with its long, yellow teeth.

Usually, I paid no attention when pigs barked and grumbled at me but this one really seemed to mean it. As I wondered what the next step would be, the pig gave an angry roar, reared up on its hind legs and tried to get over the wall at me. I made up my mind quickly.

'I'm afraid I haven't got the right instrument with me, Mr Dent. I'll pop back another day and open the ear for you. It's nothing serious – only a small job. Goodbye.'

There the matter had rested, with nobody caring to mention it till now.

Tristan was aghast. 'You mean you want me to go along there tonight. Saturday night? Surely some other time would do? I'm going to a dance.'

Siegfried smiled bitterly from the depths of his chair. 'It has to be done now. That's an order. You can go to your dance afterwards.'

Tristan started to say something, but he knew he had pushed his luck far enough. 'Right,' he said, 'I'll go and do it.'

He left the room with dignity, Siegfried resumed his book, and I stared into the fire, wondering how Tristan was going to handle this one. He was a lad of infinite resource, but he was going to be tested this time.

Within ten minutes he was back. Siegfried looked at him suspiciously. 'Have you opened that ear?'

'No.'

'Why not?'

'Couldn't find the place. You must have given me the wrong address. Number 98, you said.'

155

'It's number 89 and you know damn well it is. Now get back there and do your job.'

The door closed behind Tristan and again, I waited. Fifteen minutes later it opened again and Tristan reappeared looking faintly triumphant. His brother looked up from his book.

'Done it?'

'No.'

'Why not?'

'The family are all out at the pictures. Saturday night, you know.'

'I don't care a damn where the family are. Just get into that sty and lance that ear. Now get out, and this time I want the job done.'

Again Tristan retreated and a new vigil began. Siegfried did not say a word, but I could feel the tension building up. Twenty minutes passed and Tristan was with us again.

'Have you opened that ear?'

'No.'

'Why not?'

'It's pitch dark in there. How do you expect me to work? I've only got two hands – one for the knife and one for the torch. How can I hold the ear?'

Siegfried had been keeping a tight hold on himself, but now his control snapped. 'Don't give me any more of your bloody excuses,' he shouted, leaping from his chair. 'I don't care how you do it, but, by God, you are going to open that pig's ear tonight or I've finished with you. Now get the hell out of here and don't come back till it's done!'

My heart bled for Tristan. He had been dealt a poor hand and had played his cards with rare skill, but he had nothing left now. He stood silent in the doorway for a few moments, then he turned and walked out.

The next hour was a long one. Siegfried seemed to be enjoying his book and I even tried to read myself; but I got no meaning out of the words and it made my head ache to sit staring at them. It would have helped if I could have paced up and down the carpet but that was pretty well impossible in Siegfried's presence. I had just decided to excuse myself and go out for a walk when I heard the outer door open, then Tristan's footsteps in the passage.

A moment later, the man of destiny entered but the penetrating smell of pig got into the room just ahead of him, and as he walked over to the fire, pungent waves seemed to billow round him. Pig muck was spattered freely over his nice suit, and on his clean collar, his face and hair. There was a great smear of the stuff on the seat of his trousers but despite his ravaged appearance he still maintained his poise.

Siegfried pushed his chair back hurriedly but did not change expression.

'Have you got that ear opened?' he asked quietly.

'Yes.'

Siegfried returned to his book without comment. It seemed that the matter was closed and Tristan, after staring briefly at his brother's bent head, turned and marched from the room. But even after he had gone, the odour of the pigsty hung in the room like a cloud.

Later, in the Drovers', I watched Tristan draining his third pint. He had changed, and if he didn't look as impressive as when he started the evening, at least he was clean and hardly smelt at all. I had said nothing yet, but the old light was returning to his eye. I went over to the bar and ordered my second half and Tristan's fourth pint and, as I set the glasses on the table, I thought that perhaps it was time.

'Well, what happened?'

Tristan took a long, contented pull at his glass and lit a Woodbine. 'Well now, all in all, Jim, it was rather a smooth operation, but I'll start at the beginning. You can imagine me standing all alone outside the sty in the pitch darkness with that bloody great pig grunting and growling on the other side of the wall. I didn't feel so good, I can tell you.

'I shone my torch on the thing's face and it jumped up and ran at me, making a noise like a lion and showing all those dirty yellow teeth. I nearly wrapped it up and came home there and then, but I got to thinking about the dance and all and, on the spur of the moment, I hopped over the wall.

'Two seconds later, I was on my back. It must have charged me but couldn't see enough to get a bite in. I just heard a bark, then a terrific weight against my legs and I was down.

'Well, it's a funny thing, Jim. You know I'm not a violent chap, but as I lay there, all my fears vanished and all I felt was a cold hatred of that bloody animal. I saw it as the cause of all my troubles and before I knew what I was doing I was up on my feet and booting its arse round and round the sty. And, do you know, it showed no fight at all. That pig was a coward at heart.'

I was still puzzled. 'But the ear – how did you manage to open the haematoma?'

'No problem, Jim. That was done for me.'

'You don't mean to say . . .'

'Yes,' Tristan said, holding his pint up to the light and studying a small foreign body floating in the depths. 'Yes, it was really very fortunate. In the scuffle in the dark, the pig ran up against the wall and burst the thing itself. Made a beautiful job.'

CHAPTER TWENTY-FIVE

I realized, quite suddenly, that spring had come. It was late March and I had been examining some sheep in a hillside fold. On my way down, in the lee of a small pine wood I leaned my back against a tree and was aware, all at once, of the sunshine, warm on my closed eyelids, the clamour of the larks, the muted sea-sound of the wind in the high branches. And though the snow still lay in long runnels behind the walls and the grass was lifeless and winter-yellowed, there was the feeling of change; almost of liberation, because, unknowing, I had surrounded myself with a carapace against the iron months, the relentless cold.

It wasn't a warm spring but it was dry with sharp winds which fluttered the white heads of the snowdrops and bent the clumps of daffodils on the village greens. In April the roadside banks were bright with the fresh yellow of the primroses.

And in April, too, came the lambing. It came in a great tidal wave, the most vivid and interesting part of the veterinary surgeon's year, the zenith of the annual cycle, and it came as it always does when we were busiest with our other work.

In the spring the livestock were feeling the effects of the long winter. Cows had stood for months in the same few feet of byre and were in dire need of the green grass and the sun on their backs, while their calves had very little resistance to disease. And just when we were wondering how we could cope with the coughs and colds and pneumonias and acetonaemias the wave struck us.

The odd thing is that for about ten months of the year, sheep hardly entered into the scheme of our lives. They were just woolly things on the hills. But for the other two months they almost blotted out everything else.

First came the early troubles, the pregnancy toxaemias, the prolapses. Then the lambings in a concentrated rush followed by the calcium deficiencies, the horrible gangrenous mastitis when the udder turns black and sloughs away; and the diseases which beset the lambs themselves – swayback, pulpy kidney, dysentery. Then the flood slackened, became a trickle and by the end of May had almost dried up. Sheep became woolly things on the hills again.

But in this first year I found a fascination in the work which has remained with me. Lambing, it seemed to me, had all the thrill and interest of calving without the hard labour. It was usually uncomfortable in that it was performed in the open; either in draughty pens improvised from straw bales and gates or more often out in the fields. It didn't seem to occur to the farmers that the ewe might prefer to produce her family in a warm place or that the vet may not enjoy kneeling for an hour in his shirt sleeves in the rain.

But the actual job was as easy as a song. After my experiences in correcting the malpresentations of calves it was delightful to manipulate these tiny creatures. Lambs are usually born in twos or threes and some wonderful mix-ups occur; tangles of heads and legs all trying to be first out and it is the vet's job to sort them around and decide which leg belonged to which head. I revelled in this. It was a pleasant change to be for once stronger and bigger than my patient, but I didn't over-stress this advantage; I have not changed the opinion I formed then that there are just two things to remember in lambing – cleanliness and gentleness.

And the lambs. All young animals are appealing but the lamb has been given an unfair share of charm. The moments come back; of a bitterly cold evening when I had delivered twins on a wind-scoured hillside; the lambs shaking their heads convulsively and within minutes one of them struggling upright and making its way, unsteady, knock-kneed, towards the udder while the other followed resolutely on its knees.

The shepherd, his purpled, weather-roughened face almost hidden by the heavy coat which muffled him to his ears, gave a slow chuckle. 'How the 'ell do they know?'

He had seen it happen thousands of times and he still wondered. So do I.

And another memory of two hundred lambs in a barn on a warm afternoon. We were inoculating them against pulpy kidney and there was no conversation because of the high pitched protests of the lambs and the unremitting deep baa-ing from nearly a hundred ewes milling anxiously around outside. I couldn't conceive how these ewes could ever get their own families sorted out from that mass of almost identical little creatures. It would take hours.

It took about twenty-five seconds. When we had finished injecting we opened the barn doors and the outpouring lambs were met by a concerted rush of distraught mothers. At first the noise was deafening but it died away rapidly to an occasional bleat as the last stray was rounded up. Then, neatly paired off, the flock headed calmly for the field.

Through May and early June my world became softer and warmer. The cold wind dropped and the air, fresh as the sea, carried a faint breath of the thousands of wild flowers which speckled the pastures. At times it seemed unfair that I should be paid for my work; for driving out in the early morning with the fields glittering under the first pale sunshine and the wisps of mist hanging on the high tops.

At Skeldale House the wistaria exploded into a riot of mauve blooms which thrust themselves through the open windows and each morning as I shaved I breathed in the heady fragrance from the long clusters drooping by the side of the mirror. Life was idyllic.

There was only one jarring note; it was the time of the horse. In the thirties there were still quite a lot of horses on the farms though the tractors had already sounded their warning knell. In the farms near the foot of the Dale where there was a fair amount of arable land the rows of stables were half empty but there were still enough horses to make May and June uncomfortable. This was when the castrations were done.

Before that came the foaling and it was a common enough thing to see a mare with her foal either trotting beside her or stretched flat on the ground as its mother nibbled at the grass. Nowadays the sight of a cart mare and foal in a field would make me pull up my car to have another look.

There was all the work connected with the foalings; cleansing the mares, docking the foals' tails, treating the illnesses of the new born – joint ill, retained meconium. It was hard and interesting but as the weather grew warmer the farmers began to think of having the year old colts castrated.

I didn't like the job and since there might be up to a hundred to be done, it cast a shadow over this and many subsequent springs. For generations the operation had been done by casting the colt and tying him up very like a trussed chicken. It was a bit laborious but the animal was under complete restraint and it was possible to concentrate entirely on the job; but at about the time I qualified, standing castration was coming very much to the fore. It consisted simply of applying a twitch to the colt's upper lip, injecting a shot of local anaesthetic into each testicle and going straight ahead. There was no doubt it was a lot quicker.

The obvious disadvantage was that the danger of injury to the operator and his helpers was increased tenfold, but for all that the method rapidly became more popular. A local farmer called Kenny Bright who considered himself an advanced thinker took the step of introducing it to the district. He engaged Major Farley, the horse specialist, to give a demonstration on one of his colts, and a large gathering of farmers came to spectate. Kenny, smug and full of self importance was holding the twitch and beaming round the company as his protégé prepared to disinfect the operation site, but as soon as the Major touched the scrotum with his antiseptic the colt reared and brought a fore foot crashing down on Kenny's head. He was carried away on a gate with his skull fractured and spent a long time in hospital. The other farmers didn't stop laughing for weeks but the example failed to deter them. Standing castration was in.

I said it was quicker. It was when everything went smoothly, but there were other times when the colt kicked or threw himself on top of us or just went generally mad. Out of ten jobs nine would be easy and the tenth would be a rodeo. I don't know how much apprehension this state of affairs built up in other vets but I was undeniably tense on castration mornings.

Of course, one of the reasons was that I was not, am not and never will be a horseman. It is difficult to define the term but I am convinced that horsemen are either born or acquire the talent in early childhood. I knew it was no good my trying to start in my mid twenties. I had the knowledge of equine diseases, I believed I had the ability to treat sick horses efficiently but that power the real horseman had to sooth and quieten and mentally dominate an animal was beyond my reach. I didn't even try to kid myself.

It was unfortunate because there is no doubt horses know. It is quite different with cows; they don't care either way; if a cow feels like kicking you she will kick you; she doesn't give a damn whether you are an expert or not. But horses know.

So on those mornings my morale was never very high as I drove out with my instruments rattling and rolling about on an enamel tray on the back seat. Would he be wild or quiet? How big would he be? I had heard my colleagues airily stating their preference for big horses – the two year olds were far easier, they said, you could get a better grip on the testicles. But there was never any doubt in my own mind. I liked them small; the smaller the better.

One morning when the season was at its height and I had had about enough of the equine race, Siegfried called to me as he was going out. 'James, there's a horse with a tumour on its belly at Wilkinson's of White Cross. Get along and take it off – today if possible but otherwise fix your own time; I'll leave it with you.'

Feeling a little disgruntled at fate having handed me something on top of the seasonal tasks, I boiled up a scalpel, tumour spoons and syringe and put them on my tray with local anaesthetic, iodine and tetanus antitoxin.

I drove to the farm with the tray rattling ominously behind me. That sound always had a connotation of doom for me. I wondered about the horse – maybe it was just a yearling; they did get those little dangling growths sometimes – nanberries, the farmers called them. Over the six miles I managed to build up a comfortable picture of a soft-eyed little colt with pendulous abdomen and over-long hair; it hadn't done well over the winter and was probably full of worms – shaky on its legs with weakness, in fact.

At Wilkinson's all was quiet. The yard was empty except for a lad of about ten who didn't know where the boss was.

'Well, where is the horse?' I asked.

The lad pointed to the stable. 'He's in there.'

I went inside. At one end stood a high, open-topped loose box with a metal grill topping the wooden walls and from within I heard a deep-throated whinnying and snorting followed by a series of tremendous thuds against the sides of the box. A chill crept through me. That was no little colt in there.

I opened the top half door and there, looking down at me was an enormous animal; I hadn't realized horses ever came quite as big as this; a chestnut stallion with a proud arch to his neck and feet like manhole covers. Surging swathes of muscle shone on his shoulders and quarters and when he saw me he laid back his ears, showed the whites of his eyes and lashed out viciously against the wall. A foot long splinter flew high in the air as the great hoof crashed against the boards.

'God almighty,' I breathed and closed the half door hurriedly. I leaned my back against the door and listened to my heart thumping.

I turned to the lad. 'How old is that horse?'

'Over six years, sir.'

I tried a little calm thinking. How did you go about tackling a man-eater like this. I had never seen such a horse – he must weigh over a ton. I shook myself; I hadn't even had a look at the tumour I was supposed to remove. I lifted the latch, opened the door about two inches and peeped inside. I could see it plainly dangling from the belly; probably a papilloma, about the size of a cricket ball, with a lobulated surface which made it look like a little cauliflower. It swung gently from side to side as the horse moved about.

No trouble to take it off. Nice narrow neck to it; a few cc's of local in there and I could twist it off easily with the spoons.

But the snag was obvious. I would have to go under that shining barrel of an abdomen within easy reach of the great feet and stick a needle into those few inches of skin. Not a happy thought.

But I pulled my mind back to practical things; like a bucket of hot water, soap and a towel. And I'd need a good man on the twitch. I began to walk towards the house.

There was no answer to my knock. I tried again; still nothing – there was nobody at home. It seemed the most natural thing in the world to leave everything till another day; the idea of going round the buildings and fields till I found somebody never entered my head.

I almost broke into a gallop on my way to the car, backed it round with the tyres squealing and roared out of the yard.

Siegfried was surprised. 'Nobody there? Well that's a damn funny thing. I'm nearly sure they were expecting you today. But never mind, it's in your hands, James. Give them a ring and fix it up again as soon as possible.'

I found it wonderfully easy to forget about the stallion over the days and weeks that followed; except when my defences were down. At least once a night it thundered through my dreams with gaping nostrils and flying mane and I developed an uncomfortable habit of coming bolt awake at five o'clock in the morning and starting immediately to operate on the horse. On an average, I took that tumour off twenty times before breakfast each morning.

I told myself it would be a lot easier to fix the job up and get it over. What was I waiting for, anyway? Was there a subconscious hope that if I put it off long enough something would happen to get me off the hook? The tumour might fall off or shrink away and disappear, or the horse might drop down dead.

I could have passed the whole thing on to Siegfried – he was good with horses – but my confidence was low enough without that.

All my doubts were resolved one morning when Mr Wilkinson came on the phone. He wasn't in the least upset at the long delay but he made it quite clear that he could wait no longer. 'You see, I want to sell this 'oss, young man, but I can't let him go with that thing on him, can I?'

My journey to Wilkinson's wasn't enlivened by the familiar clatter of the tray on the back seat; it reminded me of the last time when I was wondering what was ahead of me. This time I knew.

Stepping out of the car, I felt almost disembodied. It was like walking a few inches above the ground. I was greeted by a reverberating din from the loose box; the same angry whinneys and splintering crashes I had heard before. I tried to twist my stiff face into a smile as the farmer came over.

'My chaps are getting a halter on him,' he said, but his words were cut short by an enraged squealing from the box and two tremendous blows against the wooden sides. I felt my mouth going dry.

The noise was coming nearer; then the stable doors flew open and the great horse catapulted out into the yard, dragging two big fellows along on the end of the halter shank. The cobbles struck sparks from the men's boots as they slithered about but they were unable to stop the stallion backing and plunging. I imagined I could feel the ground shudder under my feet as the hooves crashed down.

At length, after much manoeuvring, the men got the horse standing with his off side against the wall of the barn. One of them looped the twitch on to the upper lip and tightened it expertly, the other took a firm grip on the halter and turned towards me. 'Ready for you now, sir.'

I pierced the rubber cap on the bottle of cocaine, withdrew the plunger of the syringe and watched the clear fluid flow into the glass barrel. Seven, eight, ten cc's. If I could get that in, the rest would be easy; but my hands were trembling.

Walking up to the horse was like watching an action from a film. It wasn't really me doing this – the whole thing was unreal. The near side eye flickered dangerously at me as I raised my left hand and passed it over the muscles of the neck, down the smooth, quivering flank and along the abdomen till I was able to grasp the tumour. I had the thing in my hand now, the lobulations firm and lumpy under my fingers. I pulled gently downwards, stretching the brown skin joining the growth to the body. I would put the local in there – a few good weals. It wasn't going to be so bad. The stallion laid back his ears and gave a warning whicker.

I took a long, careful breath, brought up the syringe with my right hand, placed the needle against the skin then thrust it in.

The kick was so explosively quick that at first I felt only surprise that such a huge animal could move so swiftly. It was a lightning outward slash that I never even saw and the hoof struck the inside of my right thigh, spinning me round helplessly. When I hit the ground I lay still, feeling only a curious numbness. Then I tried to move and a stab of pain went through my leg.

When I opened my eyes Mr Wilkinson was bending over me. 'Are you all right, Mr Herriot?' The voice was anxious.

'I don't think so.' I was astonished at the matter of fact sound of my own words; but stranger still was the feeling of being at peace with myself for the first time for weeks. I was calm and completely in charge of the situation.

'I'm afraid not, Mr Wilkinson. You'd better put the horse back in his box for now – we'll have a go at him another day – and I wonder if you'd ring Mr Farnon to come and pick me up. I don't think I'll be able to drive.'

My leg wasn't broken but it developed a massive haematoma at the point of impact and then the whole limb blossomed into an unbelievable range of colours from delicate orange to deepest black. I was still hobbling like a Crimean veteran when, a fortnight later, Siegfried and I with a small army of helpers went back and roped the stallion, chloroformed him and removed that little growth.

I have a cavity in the muscle of my thigh to remind me of that day, but some good came out of the incident. I found that the fear is worse than the reality and horse work has never worried me as much since then.

CHAPTER TWENTY-SIX

The first time I saw Phin Calvert was in the street outside the surgery when I was talking to Brigadier Julian Coutts-Browne about his shooting dogs. The Brigadier was almost a stage version of an English aristocrat; immensely tall with a pronounced stoop, hawk features and a high drawling voice. As he spoke, smoke from a narrow cigar trickled from his lips.

I turned my head at the clatter of heavy boots on the pavement. A thick set figure was stumping rapidly towards us, hands tucked behind his braces, ragged jacket pulled wide to display a curving expanse of collarless shirt, wisps of grizzled hair hanging in a fringe beneath a greasy cap. He was smiling widely at nobody in particular and he hummed busily to himself.

The Brigadier glanced at him. 'Morning, Calvert,' he grunted coldly.

Phineas threw up his head in pleased recognition. 'Now then, Charlie, 'ow is ta?' he shouted.

The Brigadier looked as though he had swallowed a swift pint of vinegar. He removed his cigar with a shaking hand and stared after the retreating back. 'Impudent devil,' he muttered.

Looking at Phin, you would never have thought he was a prosperous farmer. I was called to his place a week later and was surprised to find a substantial house and buildings and a fine dairy herd grazing in the fields.

I could hear him even before I got out of the car.

'Hello, 'ello, 'ello! Who's this we've got then? New chap eh? Now we're going to learn summat!' He still had his hands inside his braces and was grinning wider than ever.

'My name is Herriot,' I said.

'Is it now?' Phin cocked his head and surveyed me, then he

168

turned to three young men standing by. 'Hasn't he a nice smile, lads. He's a real Happy Harry!'

He turned and began to lead the way across the yard. 'Come on, then and we'll see what you're made of. I 'ope you know a bit about calves because I've got some here that are right dowly.'

As he went into the calf house I was hoping I would be able to do something impressive – perhaps use some of the new drugs and sera I had in my car; it was going to take something special to make an impact here.

There were six well grown young animals, almost stirk size, and three of them were behaving very strangely; grinding their teeth, frothing at the mouth and blundering about the pen as though they couldn't see. As I watched, one of them walked straight into the wall and stood with its nose pressed against the stone.

Phin, apparently unconcerned, was humming to himself in a corner. When I started to take my thermometer from its case he burst into a noisy commentary. 'Now what's he doing? Ah, we're off now, get up there!'

The half minute which my thermometer spends in an animal's rectum is usually devoted to hectic thought. But this time I didn't need the time to work out my diagnosis; the blindness made it easy. I began to look round the walls of the calf house; it was dark and I had to get my face close to the stone.

Phin gave tongue again. 'Hey, what's going on? You're as bad as t' calves, nosing about there, dozy like. What d'you think you're lookin' for?'

'Paint, Mr Calvert. I'm nearly sure your calves have got lead poisoning.'

Phin said what all farmers say at this juncture. 'They can't have. I've had calves in here for thirty years and they've never taken any harm before. There's no paint in here, anyway.'

'How about this, then?' I peered into the darkest corner and pulled at a piece of loose board.

'Oh, that's nobbut a bit of wood I nailed down there last week to block up a hole. Came off an old hen house.'

I looked at the twenty year old paint hanging off in the loose flakes which calves find so irresistible. 'This is what's done the damage,' I said. 'Look, you can see the tooth marks where they've been at it.'

Phin studied the board at close quarters and grunted doubtfully. 'All right, what do we do now?'

'First thing is to get this painted board out of here and then give all the calves epsom salts. Have you got any?'

Phin gave a bark of laughter. 'Aye, I've got a bloody great sack full, but can't you do owt better than that? Aren't you going to inject them?'

It was a little embarrassing. The specific antidotes to metal poisoning had not been discovered and the only thing which sometimes did a bit of good was magnesium sulphate which caused the precipitation of insoluble lead sulphate. The homely term for magnesium sulphate is of course, epsom salts.

'No,' I said. 'There's nothing I can inject that will help at all and I can't even guarantee the salts will. But I'd like you to give the calves two heaped tablespoonfuls three times a day.'

'Oh 'ell, you'll skitter the poor buggers to death!'

'Maybe so, but there's nothing else for it,' I said.

Phin took a step towards me so that his face, dark-skinned and deeply wrinkled, was close to mine. The suddenly shrewd, mottled brown eyes regarded me steadily for a few seconds then he turned away quickly. 'Right,' he said. 'Come in and have a drink.'

Phin stumped into the farm kitchen ahead of me, threw back his head and let loose a bellow that shook the windows. 'Mother! Feller 'ere wants a glass o' beer. Come and meet Happy Harry!'

Mrs Calvert appeared with magical speed and put down glasses and bottles. I glanced at the labels – 'Smith's Nutty Brown Ale', and filled my glass. It was a historic moment though I didn't know it then; it was the first of an incredible series of Nutty Browns I was to drink at that table.

Mrs Calvert sat down for a moment, crossed her hands on her lap and smiled encouragingly. 'Can you do anything for the calves, then?' she asked.

Phin butted in before I could reply. 'Oh aye, he can an' all. He's put them on to epsom salts.'

'Epsom salts?'

'That's it, Missis. I said when he came that we'd get summat real smart and scientific like. You can't beat new blood and modern ideas.' Phin sipped his beer gravely.

Over the following days the calves gradually improved and at the end of a fortnight they were all eating normally. The worst one still showed a trace of blindness, but I was confident this too would clear up.

It wasn't long before I saw Phin again. It was early afternoon and I was in the office with Siegfried when the outer door banged and the passage echoed to the clumping of hob nails. I heard a voice raised in song – hi-ti-tiddly-rum-te-tum. Phineas was in our midst once more.

'Well, well, well!' he bawled heartily at Miss Harbottle. 'It's Flossie! And what's my little darlin' doing this fine day?'

There was not a flicker from Miss Harbottle's granite features. She directed an icy stare at the intruder but Phin swung round on Siegfried with a yellow-toothed grin. 'Now, gaffer, 'ow's tricks?'

'Everything's fine, Mr Calvert,' Siegfried replied. 'What can we do for you?'

Phin stabbed a finger at me. 'There's my man. I want him out to my place right sharpish.'

'What's the trouble?' I asked. 'Is it the calves again?'

'Damn, no! Wish it was. It's me good bull. He's puffin' like a bellows – bit like pneumonia but worse than I've known. He's in a 'ell of a state. Looks like he's peggin' out.' For an instant Phin lost his jocularity.

I had heard of this bull; pedigree shorthorn, show winner,

171

the foundation of his herd. 'I'll be right after you, Mr Calvert. I'll follow you along.'

'Good lad. I'm off, then.' Phin paused at the door, a wild figure, tireless, tattered; baggy trousers ballooning from his ample middle. He turned again to Miss Harbottle and contorted his leathery features into a preposterous leer. 'Ta-ra, Floss!' he cried and was gone.

For a moment the room seemed very empty and quiet except for Miss Harbottle's acid 'Oh, that man! Dreadful! Dreadful!'

I made good time to the farm and found Phin waiting with his three sons. The young men looked gloomy but Phin was still indomitable. 'Here 'e is!' he shouted. 'Happy Harry again. Now we'll be all right.' He even managed a little tune as we crossed to the bull pen but when he looked over the door his head sank on his chest and his hands worked deeper behind his braces.

The bull was standing as though rooted to the middle of the pen. His great rib cage rose and fell with the most laboured respirations I had ever seen. His mouth gaped wide, a bubbling foam hung round his lips and his flaring nostrils; his eyes, almost starting from his head in terror, stared at the wall in front of him. This wasn't pneumonia, it was a frantic battle for breath; and it looked like a losing one.

He didn't move when I inserted my thermometer and though my mind was racing I suspected the half minute wasn't going to be long enough this time. I had expected accelerated breathing, but nothing like this.

'Poor aud beggar,' Phin muttered. 'He's bred me the finest calves I've ever had and he's quiet as a sheep, too. I've seen me little grandchildren walk under 'is belly and he's took no notice. I hate to see him sufferin' like this. If you can't do no good, just tell me and I'll get the gun out.'

I took the thermometer out and read it. One hundred and ten degrees fahrenheit. This was ridiculous; I shook it vigorously and pushed it back into the rectum.

I gave it nearly a minute this time so that I could get in some extra thinking. The second reading said a hundred and ten again and I had an unpleasant conviction that if the thermometer had been a foot long the mercury would still have been jammed against the top.

What in the name of God was this? Could be Anthrax ... must be ... and yet ... I looked over at the row of heads above the half door; they were waiting for me to say something and their silence accentuated the agonized groaning and panting. I looked above the heads to the square of deep blue and a tufted cloud moving across the sun. As it passed, a single dazzling ray made me close my eyes and a faint bell rang in my mind.

'Has he been out today?' I asked.

'Aye, he's been out on the grass on his tether all morning. It was that grand and warm.'

The bell became a triumphant gong. 'Get a hosepipe in here quick. You can rig it to that tap in the yard.'

'A hosepipe? What the 'ell ...?'

'Yes, quick as you can – he's got sunstroke.'

They had the hose fixed in less than a minute. I turned it full on and began to play the jet of cold water all over the huge form – his face and neck, along the ribs, up and down the legs. I kept this up for about five minutes but it seemed a lot longer as I waited for some sign of improvement. I was beginning to think I was on the wrong track when the bull gulped just once.

It was something – he had been unable to swallow his saliva before in his desperate efforts to get the air into his lungs; and I really began to notice a change in the big animal. Surely he was looking just a little less distressed and wasn't the breathing slowing down a bit?

Then the bull shook himself, turned his head and looked at us. There was an awed whisper from one of the young men: 'By gaw, it's working!'

I enjoyed myself after that. I can't think of anything in my working life that has given me more pleasure than standing in that pen directing the life-saving jet and watching the bull savouring it. He liked it on his face best and as I worked my way up from the tail and along the steaming back he would turn his nose full into the water, rocking his head from side to side and blinking blissfully.

Within half an hour he looked almost normal. His chest was still heaving a little but he was in no discomfort. I tried the temperature again. Down to a hundred and five.

'He'll be all right now,' I said, 'but I think one of the lads should keep the water on him for another twenty minutes or so. I'll have to go now.'

'You've time for a drink,' Phin grunted.

In the farm kitchen his bellow of 'Mother' lacked some of its usual timbre. He dropped into a chair and stared into his glass of Nutty Brown. 'Harry,' he said, 'I'll tell you, you've flummoxed me this time.' He sighed and rubbed his chin in apparent disbelief. 'I don't know what the 'ell to say to you.'

It wasn't often that Phin lost his voice, but he found it again very soon at the next meeting of the farmers' discussion group.

A learned and earnest gentleman had been expounding on the advances in veterinary medicine and how the farmers could now expect their stock to be treated as the doctors treated their human patients, with the newest drugs and procedures.

It was too much for Phin. He jumped to his feet and cried: 'Ah think you're talking a lot of rubbish. There's a young feller in Darrowby not long out of college and it doesn't matter what you call 'im out for he uses nowt but epsom salts and cold water.'

CHAPTER TWENTY-SEVEN

It was during one of Siegfried's efficiency drives that Colonel Merrick's cow picked up a wire. The colonel was a personal friend, which made things even more uncomfortable.

Everybody suffered when Siegfried had these spells. They usually came on after he had been reading a technical work or when he had seen a film of some new technical procedure. He would rampage around, calling on the cowering household to stir themselves and be better men. He would be obsessed, for a time, with the craving for perfection.

'We must put on a better show at these operations on the farms. It just isn't good enough to fish out a few old instruments from a bag and start hacking at the animal. We must have cleanliness, asepsis if possible, and an orderly technique.'

So he was jubilant when he diagnosed traumatic reticulitis (foreign body in the second stomach) in the colonel's cow. 'We'll really show old Hubert something. We'll give him a picture of veterinary surgery he'll never forget.'

Tristan and I were pressed into service as assistants, and our arrival at the farm was really impressive. Siegfried led the procession, looking unusually smart in a brand new tweed jacket of which he was very proud. He was a debonair figure as he shook hands with his friend.

The colonel was jovial. 'Hear you're going to operate on my cow. Take out a wire, eh? Like to watch you do it, if it's all right with you.'

'By all means, Hubert, please do. You'll find it very interesting.'

In the byre, Tristan and I had to bustle about. We arranged tables alongside the cow and on these we placed new metal trays with rows of shining, sterilized instruments. Scalpels, directors, probes, artery forceps, hypodermic syringes, suture needles, gut and silk in glass phials, rolls of cotton wool and various bottles of spirit and other antiseptics.

Siegfried fussed around, happy as a schoolboy. He had clever hands and, as a surgeon, he was worth watching. I could read his mind without much trouble. This, he was thinking, was going to be good.

When all was to his liking, he took off his jacket and donned a brilliantly white smock. He handed the jacket to Tristan and almost instantly gave a roar of anger. 'Hey, don't just throw it down on that meal bin! Here, give it to me. I'll find a safe place for it.' He dusted the new garment down tenderly and hung it on a nail on the wall.

Meanwhile, I had shaved and disinfected the operation site on the flank and everything was ready for the local anaesthetic. Siegfried took the syringe and quickly infiltrated the area. 'This is where we go inside, Hubert. I hope you aren't squeamish.'

The colonel beamed. 'Oh, I've seen blood before. You needn't worry, I shan't faint.'

With a bold sweep of the scalpel, Siegfried incised the skin, then the muscles and finally, with delicate care, the glistening peritoneum. The smooth wall of the rumen (the large first stomach) lay exposed.

Siegfried reached for a fresh scalpel and looked for the best place to cut in. But as he poised his knife, the wall of the rumen suddenly bulged out through the skin incision. 'Unusual,' he muttered. 'Probably a bit of rumenal gas.' Unflurried, he gently thrust back the protrusion and prepared again to make his cut; but as he withdrew his hand, the rumen welled out after it, a pinkish mass bigger than a football. Siegfried pushed it back and it shot out again immediately, ballooning to a startling size. This time, he took two hands to the job, pushing and pressing till he forced the thing once more out of sight. He stood for a moment with his hands inside the cow, breathing heavily. Two beads of sweat trickled down his forehead.

Carefully, he withdrew his hands. Nothing happened. It must have settled down. He was reaching back for his knife when, like a live thing, the rumen again came leaping and surging out. It seemed almost as though the entire organ had escaped through the incision – a slippery, gleaming mass rising and swelling till it was level with his eyes.

Siegfried had dropped all pretence of calm and was fighting desperately, both arms round the thing, pressing downwards with all his strength. I hastened forward to help and, as I drew near, he whispered hoarsely: 'What the hell is it?' Clearly, he was wondering if this pulsating heap of tissue was some part of the bovine anatomy he had never even heard of.

Silently, we fought the mass down till it was level with the skin. The colonel was watching intently. He hadn't expected the operation to be so interesting. His eyebrows were slightly raised.

'It must be gas that's doing this,' panted Siegfried. 'Pass me the knife and stand back.'

He inserted the knife into the rumen and cut sharply downwards. I was glad I had moved away because, through the incision shot a high pressure jet of semi-liquid stomach contents – a greenish-brown, foul-smelling cascade which erupted from the depths of the cow as from an invisible pump.

The first direct hit was on Siegfried's face. He couldn't release his hold of the rumen or it would have slipped back into the abdomen and contaminated the peritoneum. So he hung on to each side of the opening while the evil torrent poured onto his hair, down his neck and all over his lovely white smock.

Now and then, the steady stream would be varied by a sudden explosion which sent the fermenting broth spouting viciously over everything in the immediate vicinity. Within a minute, the trays with their gleaming instruments were thoroughly covered. The tidy rows of swabs, the snowy tufts of cotton wool disappeared without trace, but it was the unkindest cut of all when a particular powerful jet sent a liberal spray over the new jacket hanging on the wall. Siegfried's face was too obscured for me to detect any change of expression but at this disaster, I saw real anguish in his eyes.

The colonel's eyebrows were now raised to the maximum and his mouth hung open as he gazed in disbelief at the chaotic scene. Siegfried, still hanging grimly on, was the centre of it all, paddling about in a reeking swamp which came halfway up his Wellington boots. He looked like a Fiji Islander with his hair stiffened and frizzled and his eyes rolling whitely in the brown face.

Eventually, the flood slowed to a trickle and stopped. I was able to hold the lips of the wound while Siegfried inserted his arm and felt his way to the reticulum. I watched him as he groped inside the honeycombed organ far out of sight against the diaphragm. A satisfied grunt told me he had located the piercing wire and within seconds he had removed it.

Tristan had been frantically salvaging and washing suture materials and soon the incision in the rumen was stitched. Siegfried's heroic stand had not been in vain; there was no contamination of the peritoneum.

Silently and neatly, he secured the skin and muscles with retention sutures and swabbed round the wound. Everything looked fine. The cow seemed unperturbed; under the anaesthetic she had known nothing of the titanic struggle with her insides. In fact, freed from the discomfort of the transfixing wire, she appeared already to be feeling better.

It took quite a time to tidy up the mess and the most difficult job was to make Siegfried presentable. We did our best by swilling him down with buckets of water while, all the time, he scraped sadly at his new jacket with a flat stick. It didn't make much difference.

The colonel was hearty and full of congratulations. 'Come in, my dear chap. Come in and have a drink.' But the invitation had a hollow ring and he took care to stand at least ten feet away from his friend.

Siegfried threw his bedraggled jacket over his shoulder. 'No

thank you, Hubert. It's most kind of you, but we must be off.'
He went out of the byre. 'I think you'll find the cow will be
eating in a day or two. I'll be back in a fortnight to take out
the stitches.'

In the confined space of the car, Tristan and I were unable
to get as far away from him as we could have liked. Even with
our heads stuck out of the windows it was still pretty bad.

Siegfried drove for a mile or two in silence, then he turned
to me and his streaked features broke into a grin. There was
something indomitable about him. 'You never know what's
round the corner in this game, my boys, but just think of this
– that operation was a success.'

CHAPTER TWENTY-EIGHT

There were three of us in the cheerless yard, Isaac Cranford,
Jeff Mallock and myself. The only one who looked at ease was
Mallock and it was fitting that it should be so, since he was, in
a manner of speaking, the host. He owned the knacker yard
and he looked on benignly as we peered into the carcass of the
cow he had just opened.

In Darrowby the name Mallock had a ring of doom. It was
the graveyard of livestock, of farmers' ambitions, of veterinary surgeons' hopes. If ever an animal was very ill somebody
was bound to say: 'I reckon she'll be off to Mallock's afore
long,' or 'Jeff Mallock'll have 'er in t' finish.' And the premises
fitted perfectly into the picture; a group of drab, red-brick
buildings standing a few fields back from the road with a
stumpy chimney from which rolled endlessly a dolorous black
smoke.

It didn't pay to approach Mallock's too closely unless you
had a strong stomach, so the place was avoided by the towns-
people, but if you ventured up the lane and peeped through the
sliding metal doors you could look in on a nightmare world.

Dead animals lay everywhere. Most of them were dismembered and great chunks of meat hung on hooks, but here and there you could see a bloated sheep or a greenish, swollen pig which not even Jeff could bring himself to open.

Skulls and dry bones were piled to the roof in places and brown mounds of meat stood in the corners. The smell was bad at any time but when Jeff was boiling up the carcasses it was indescribable. The Mallock family bungalow stood in the middle of the buildings and strangers could be pardoned if they expected a collection of wizened gnomes to dwell there. But Jeff was a pink-faced, cherubic man in his forties, his wife plump, smiling and comely. Their family ranged from a positively beautiful girl of nineteen down to a robust five year old boy. There were eight young Mallocks and they had spent their lifetimes playing among tuberculous lungs and a vast spectrum of bacteria from Salmonella to Anthrax. They were the healthiest children in the district.

It was said in the pubs that Jeff was one of the richest men in the town but the locals, as they supped their beer, had to admit that he earned his money. At any hour of the day or night he would rattle out into the country in his ramshackle lorry, winch on a carcass, bring it back to the yard and cut it up. A dog food dealer came twice a week from Brawton with a van and bought the fresh meat. The rest of the stuff Jeff shovelled into his boiler to make the meat meal which was in great demand for mixing in pig and poultry rations. The bones went for making fertilizer, the hides to the tanner and the nameless odds and ends were collected by a wild-eyed individual known only as the 'ket feller'. Sometimes, for a bit of variety, Jeff would make long slabs of strange-smelling soap which found a brisk sale for scrubbing shop floors. Yes, people said, there was no doubt Jeff did all right. But, by gaw, he earned it.

My contacts with Mallock were fairly frequent. A knacker's yard had a useful function for a vet. It served as a crude post mortem room, a place where he could check on his diagnosis in fatal cases; and on occasions where he had been completely baffled, the mysteries would be revealed under Jeff's knife.

Often, of course, farmers would send in an animal which I had been treating and ask Jeff to tell them 'what had been wrong wi't' and this was where a certain amount of friction arose. Because Jeff was placed in a position of power and seldom resisted the temptation to wield it. Although he could neither read nor write, he was a man of great professional pride; he didn't like to be called a knacker man but preferred 'fell-monger'. He considered in his heart that, after twenty odd years of cutting up diseased animals he knew more than any vet alive, and it made things rather awkward that the farming community unhesitatingly agreed with him.

It never failed to spoil my day if a farmer called in at the surgery and told me that, once more, Jeff Mallock had confounded my diagnosis. 'Hey, remember that cow you were treating for magnesium deficiency? She never did no good and ah sent 'er into Mallocks. Well, you know what was really the matter wi' 'er? Worm i' the tail. Jeff said if you'd nobbut cut tail off, that cow would have gotten up and walked away.' It was no good arguing or saying there was no such thing as worm in the tail. Jeff knew – that was all about it.

If only Jeff had taken his priceless opportunities to acquire a commonsense knowledge it wouldn't have been so bad. But instead, he had built up a weird pathology of his own and backed it up by black magic remedies gleaned from his contacts with the more primitive members of the farming community. His four stock diseases were Stagnation of t'lungs, Black Rot, Gastric Ulsters and Golf Stones. It was a quartet which made the vets tremble for miles around.

Another cross which the vets had to bear was his unique gift of being able to take one look at a dead animal on a farm and pronounce immediately on the cause of death. The farmers, awe-struck by his powers, were always asking me why I couldn't do it. But I was unable to dislike the man. He would have had to be more than human to resist the chance to be important and there was no malice in his actions. Still, it made things uncomfortable at times and I liked to be on the spot myself whenever possible. Especially when Isaac Cranford was involved.

Cranford was a hard man, a man who had cast his life in a mould of iron austerity. A sharp bargainer, a win-at-all-cost character and, in a region where thrift was general, he was noted for meanness. He farmed some of the best land in the lower Dale, his Shorthorns won prizes regularly at the shows but he was nobody's friend. Mr Bateson, his neighbour to the North, summed it up: 'That feller 'ud skin a flea for its hide.' Mr Dickon, his neighbour to the South, put it differently: 'If he gets haud on a pound note, by gaw it's a prisoner.'

This morning's meeting had had its origin the previous day. A phone call mid afternoon from Mr Cranford. 'I've had a cow struck by lightning. She's laid dead in the field.'

I was surprised. 'Lightning? Are you sure? We haven't had a storm today.'

'Maybe you haven't, but we have 'ere.'

'Mmm, all right, I'll come and have a look at her.'

Driving to the farm, I couldn't work up much enthusiasm for the impending interview. This lightning business could be a bit of a headache. All farmers were insured against lightning stroke – it was usually part of their fire policy – and after a severe thunder storm it was common enough for the vets' phones to start ringing with requests to examine dead beasts.

The insurance companies were reasonable about it. If they received a certificate from the vet that he believed lightning to be the cause of death they would usually pay up without fuss. In cases of doubt they would ask for a post mortem or a second opinion from another practitioner. The difficulty was that there are no diagnostic post mortem features to go on; occasionally a bruising of the tissues under the skin, but very little else. The happiest situation was when the beast was found with the tell-tale scorch marks running from an ear down the leg to earth into the ground. Often the animal would be found under a tree which itself had obviously been blasted and torn by lightning. Diagnosis was easy then.

Ninety-nine per cent of the farmers were looking only for a square deal and if their vet found some other clear cause of death they would accept his verdict philosophically. But the odd one could be very difficult.

I had heard Siegfried tell of one old chap who had called him out to verify a lightning death. The long scorch marks on the carcass were absolutely classical and Siegfried, viewing them, had been almost lyrical. 'Beautiful, Charlie, beautiful, I've never seen more typical marks. But there's just one thing.' He put an arm round the old man's shoulder. 'What a great pity you let the candle grease fall on the skin.'

The old man looked closer and thumped a fist into his palm. 'Dang it, you're right, maister! Ah've mucked t'job up. And ah took pains ower it an' all – been on for dang near an hour.' He walked away muttering. He showed no embarrassment, only disgust at his own technological shortcomings.

But this, I thought, as the stone walls flipped past the car windows, would be very different. Cranford was in the habit of getting his own way, right or wrong, and if he didn't get it today there would be trouble.

I drove through the farm gate and along a neat tarmac road across the single field. Mr Cranford was standing motionless in the middle of the yard and I was struck, not for the first time, by the man's resemblance to a big, hungry bird. The hunched narrow shoulders, the forward-thrust, sharp-beaked face, the dark overcoat hanging loosely on the bony frame. I wouldn't have been surprised if he had spread his wings and flapped his way on to the byre roof. Instead, he nodded impatiently at me and began to hasten with short, tripping steps to a field at the back of the house.

It was a large field and the dead cow lay almost in the centre. There were no trees, no hedges, not even a small bush. My hopeful picture of the body under a stricken tree melted immediately, leaving an anxious void.

We stopped beside the cow and Mr Cranford was the first to speak. 'Bound to be lightning. Can't be owt else. Nasty storm, then this good beast dropping down dead.'

I looked at the grass around the big Shorthorn. It had been churned and torn out, leaving patches of bare earth. 'But it hasn't exactly dropped down, has it? It died in convulsions – you can see where its feet have kicked out the grass.'

'All right then, it 'ad a convulsion, but it was lightning that caused it.' Mr Cranford had fierce little eyes and they darted flitting glances at my shirt collar, macintosh belt, Wellingtons. He never could quite bring himself to look anybody in the eye.

'I doubt it, Mr Cranford. One of the signs of lightning stroke is that the beast has fallen without a struggle. Some of them even have grass in their mouths.'

'Oh, I know all about that,' Cranford snapped, his thin face flushing. 'I've been among livestock for half a century and this isn't the first beast I've seen that's been struck. They're not all t'same, you know.'

'Oh, I realize that, but, you see, this death could have been caused by so many things.'

'What sort o' things?'

'Well, Anthrax for a start, magnesium deficiency, heart trouble – there's quite a list. I really think we ought to do a post mortem to make sure.'

'Now see here, are you saying I'm trying to do summat I shouldn't?'

'Not at all. I'm only saying we should make sure before I write a certificate. We can go and see her opened at Mallock's and, believe me, if there's no other obvious cause of death you'll get the benefit of the doubt. The insurance people are pretty good about it.'

Mr Cranford's predatory features sank lower into his coat collar. He dug his hands viciously into his pockets. 'I've had vitneries at these jobs afore. Proper, experienced vitneries, too.' The little eyes flashed in the direction of my left ear.

'They've never messed about like this. What's the use of going to all that trouble? Why do you have to be so damn particular?'

Why indeed, I thought. Why make an enemy of this man? He wielded a lot of power in the district. Prominent in the local Farmers' Union, a member of every agricultural committee for miles around. He was a wealthy, successful man and, if people didn't like him they respected his knowledge and listened to him. He could do a young vet a lot of harm. Why not write the certificate and go home? This is to certify that I have examined that above mentioned animal and, in my opinion, lightning stroke was the cause of death. It would be easy and Cranford would be mollified. It would be the end of the whole thing. Why antagonize this dangerous character for nothing? Maybe it really was lightning, anyway.

I turned to face Mr Cranford, trying in vain to look into his eyes that always veered away at the last moment. 'I'm sorry, but I feel we ought to have a look inside this cow. I'll ring Mallock and ask him to pick her up and we can see her in the morning. I'll meet you there at ten o'clock. Will that be all right?'

'Reckon it'll have to be,' Cranford spat out. 'It's a piece o' nonsense, but I suppose I've got to humour you. But just let me remind you – this was a good cow, worth all of eighty pounds. I can't afford to lose that amount of money. I want my rights.'

'I'm sure you'll get them, Mr Cranford. And before I have her moved I'd better take a blood film to eliminate Anthrax.'

The farmer had been under a mounting load of pressure. As a pillar of the methodist chapel his range of language was restricted, so he vented his pent up feelings by kicking out savagely at the carcass. His toe made contact with the unyielding backbone and he hopped around on one leg for a few seconds. Then he limped off towards the house.

I was alone as I nicked the dead ear with my knife and drew a film of blood across a couple of glass slides. It hadn't been a happy session and the one tomorrow didn't hold out much more promise. I enclosed the blood films carefully in a cardboard box and set off for Skeldale House to examine them under the microscope.

So it wasn't a particularly cheerful group which assembled at the knacker yard the following morning. Even Jeff, though he preserved his usual Buddha-like expression, was, in fact, deeply offended. The account he had given me when I first arrived at the yard was fragmentary, but I could piece the scene together. Jeff, leaping from his lorry at Cranford's, sweeping the carcass with a piercing glance and making his brilliant spot diagnosis. 'Stagnation o' t'lungs. I can allus tell by the look in their eyes and the way their hair lies along t'back.' Waiting confidently for the wondering gasps, the congratulatory speeches which always followed his tour de force.

Then Mr Cranford, almost dancing with rage. 'Shut your big, stupid mouth, Mallock, tha knows nowt about it. This cow was struck by lightning and you'd better remember that.'

And now, bending my head over the carcass, I couldn't find a clue anyway. No sign of bruising when the skin was removed. The internal organs clean and normal.

I straightened up and pushed my fingers through my hair. The boiler bubbled softly, puffing out odoriferous wisps into the already highly charged atmosphere. Two dogs licked busily at a pile of meat meal.

Then a chill of horror struck through me. The dogs had competition. A little boy with golden curls was pushing a forefinger into the heap, inserting it in his mouth and sucking with rapt enjoyment.

'Look at that!' I quavered.

The knacker man's face lit up with paternal pride. 'Aye,' he said happily. 'It isn't only the four-legged 'uns wot likes my meal. Wonderful stuff – full of nourishment!'

His good humour completely restored, he struck a match

and began to puff appreciatively at a short pipe which was thickly encrusted with evidence of his grisly trade.

I dragged my attention back to the job in hand. 'Cut into the heart, will you, Jeff,' I said.

Jeff deftly sliced the big organ from top to bottom and I knew immediately that my search was over. The auricles and ventricles were almost completely occluded by a cauliflower-like mass growing from the valves. Verrucose endocarditis, common in pigs but seldom seen in cattle.

'There's what killed your cow, Mr Cranford,' I said.

Cranford aimed his nose at the heart. 'Fiddlesticks! You're not telling me them little things could kill a beast like that.'

'They're not so little. Big enough to stop the flow of blood. I'm sorry, but there's no doubt about it – your cow died of heart failure.'

'And how about lightning?'

'No sign of it, I'm afraid. You can see for yourself.'

'And what about my eighty pounds?'

'I'm truly sorry about that, but it doesn't alter the facts.'

'Facts! What facts? I've come along this morning and you've shown me nowt to make me change my opinion.'

'Well, there's nothing more I can say. It's a clear cut case.'

Mr Cranford stiffened in his perching stance. He held his hands against the front of his coat and the fingers and thumbs rubbed together unceasingly as though fondling the beloved bank notes which were slipping away from him. His face, sunk deeper in his collar, appeared still sharper in outline.

Then he turned to me and made a ghastly attempt to smile. And his eyes, trained on my lapels, tried valiantly to inch their way upwards. There was a fleeting instance when they met my gaze before flickering away in alarm.

He drew me to one side and addressed himself to my larynx. There was a wheedling note in the hoarse whisper.

'Now look here, Mr Herriot, we're both men of the world. You know as well as I do that the insurance company can afford this loss a lot better nor me. So why can't you just say it is lightning?'

'Even though I think it isn't?'

'Well, what the hangment does it matter? You can say it is, can't you? Nobody's going to know.'

I scratched my head. 'But what would bother me, Mr Cranford, is that I would know.'

'You would know?' The farmer was mystified.

'That's right. And it's no good – I can't give you a certificate for this cow and that's the end of it.'

Dismay, disbelief, frustration chased across Mr Cranford's features. 'Well, I'll tell you this. I'm not leaving the matter here. I'm going to see your boss about you.' He swung round and pointed at the cow. 'There's no sign of disease there. Trying to tell me it's all due to little things in the heart. You don't know your job – you don't even know what them things are!'

Jeff Mallock removed his unspeakable pipe from his mouth. 'But ah know. It's what ah said. Stagnation o' t'lungs is caused by milk from milk vein getting back into the body. Finally it gets to t'heart and then it's over wi't. Them's milk clots you're looking at.'

Cranford rounded on him. 'Shut up, you great gumph! You're as bad as this feller here. It was lightning killed my good cow. Lightning!' He was almost screaming. Then he controlled himself and spoke quietly to me. 'You'll hear more of this, Mr Knowledge, and I'll just tell you one thing. You'll never walk on my farm again.' He turned and hurried away with his quick-stepping gait.

I said good morning to Jeff and climbed wearily into my car. Well, everything had worked out just great. If only vetting just consisted of treating sick animals. But it didn't. There were so many other things. I started the engine and drove away.

CHAPTER TWENTY-NINE

It didn't take Mr Cranford long to make good his threat. He called at the surgery shortly after lunch the following day and Siegfried and I, enjoying a post prandial cigarette in the sitting-room, heard the jangle of the door bell. We didn't get up, because most of the farmers walked in after ringing.

The dogs, however, went into their usual routine. They had had a long run on the high moor that morning and had just finished licking out their dinner bowls. Tired and distended, they had collapsed in a snoring heap around Siegfried's feet. There was nothing they wanted more than ten minutes' peace but, dedicated as they were to their self appointed role of fierce guardians of the house, they did not hesitate. They leaped, baying, from the rug and hurled themselves into the passage.

People often wondered why Siegfried kept five dogs. Not only kept them but took them everywhere with him. Driving on his rounds it was difficult to see him at all among the shaggy heads and waving tails; and anybody approaching the car would recoil in terror from the savage barking and the bared fangs and glaring eyes framed in the windows.

'I cannot for the life of me understand,' Siegfried would declare, thumping his fist on his knee, 'why people keep dogs as pets. A dog should have a useful function. Let it be used for farm work, for shooting, for guiding; but why anybody should keep the things just hanging around the place beats me.'

It was a pronouncement he was continually making, often through a screen of flapping ears and lolling tongues as he sat in his car. His listener would look wonderingly from the huge greyhound to the tiny terrier, from the spaniel to the whippet to the Scottie; but nobody ever asked Siegfried why he kept his own dogs.

I judged that the pack fell upon Mr Cranford about the bend

of the passage and many a lesser man would have fled; but I could hear him fighting his way doggedly forward. When he came through the sitting-room door he had removed his hat and was beating the dogs off with it. It wasn't a wise move and the barking rose to a higher pitch. The man's eyes stared and his lips moved continuously, but nothing came through.

Siegfried, courteous as ever, rose and indicated a chair. His lips, too, were moving, no doubt in a few gracious words of welcome. Mr Cranford flapped his black coat, swooped across the carpet and perched. The dogs sat in a ring round him and yelled up into his face. Usually they collapsed after their exhausting performance but there was something in the look or smell of Mr Cranford that they didn't like.

Siegfried leaned back in his chair, put his fingers together and assumed a judicial expression. Now and again he nodded understandingly or narrowed his eyes as if taking an interesting point. Practically nothing could be heard from Mr Cranford but occasionally a word or phrase penetrated.

'... have a serious complaint to make ...'
'... doesn't know his job ...'
'... can't afford ... not a rich man ...'
'... these danged dogs ...'
'... won't have 'im again ...'
'... down dog, get by ...'
'... nowt but robbery ...'

Siegfried, completely relaxed and apparently oblivious of the din, listened attentively but as the minutes passed I could see the strain beginning to tell on Mr Cranford. His eyes began to start from their sockets and the veins corded on his scrawny neck as he tried to get his message across. Finally it was too much for him; he jumped up and a leaping brown tide bore him to the door. He gave a last defiant cry, lashed out again with his hat and was gone.

Pushing open the dispensary door a few weeks later, I found my boss mixing an ointment. He was working with great care, turning and returning the glutinous mass on a marble slab.

'What's this you're doing?' I asked.

Siegfried threw down his spatula and straightened his back. 'Ointment for a boar.' He looked past me at Tristan who had just come in. 'And I don't know why the hell I'm doing it when some people are sitting around on their backsides.' He indicated the spatula. 'Right, Tristan, you can have a go. When you've finished your cigarette, that is.'

His expression softened as Tristan hastily nipped out his Woodbine and began to work away on the slab. 'Pretty stiff concoction, that. Takes a bit of mixing,' Siegfried said with satisfaction, looking at his brother's bent head. 'The back of my neck was beginning to ache with it.'

He turned to me. 'By the way, you'll be interested to hear it's for your old friend Cranford. For that prize boar of his. It's got a nasty sore across its back and he's worried to death about it. Wins him a lot of money at the shows and a blemish there would be disastrous.'

'Cranford's still with us, then.'

'Yes, it's a funny thing, but we can't get rid of him. I don't like losing clients but I'd gladly make an exception of this chap. He won't have you near the place after that lightning job and he makes it very clear he doesn't think much of me either. Tells me I never do his beasts any good – says it would have been a lot better if he'd never called me. And moans like hell when he gets his bill. He's more bother than he's worth and on top of everything he gives me the creeps. But he won't leave – he damn well won't leave.'

'He knows which side his bread's buttered,' I said. 'He gets first rate service and the moaning is part of the system to keep the bills down.'

'Maybe you're right, but I wish there was a simple way to get rid of him.' He tapped Tristan on the shoulder. 'All right, don't strain yourself. That'll do. Put it into this ointment box and label it: "Apply liberally to the boar's back three times daily, working it well in with the fingers." And post it to Mr

Cranford. And while you're on, will you post this faeces sample to the laboratory at Leeds to test for Johne's disease.' He held out a treacle tin brimming with foul-smelling, liquid diarrhoea.

It was a common thing to collect such samples and send them away for Johne's tests, worm counts, etc, and there was always one thing all the samples had in common — they were very large. All that was needed for the tests was a couple of teaspoonfuls but the farmers were lavish in their quantities. They seemed pleasantly surprised that all the vet wanted was a bit of muck from the dung channel; they threw aside their natural caution and shovelled the stuff up cheerfully into the biggest container they could find. They brushed aside all pro-tests; 'take plenty, we've lots of it' was their attitude.

Tristan took hold of the tin gingerly and began to look along the shelves. 'We don't seem to have any of those little glass sample jars.'

'That's right, we're out of them,' said Siegfried. 'I meant to order some more. But never mind — shove the lid on that tin and press it down tight, then parcel it up well in brown paper. It'll travel to the lab all right.'

It took only three days for Mr Cranford's name to come up again. Siegfried was opening the morning mail, throwing the circulars to one side and making a pile of the bills and receipts when he became suddenly very still. He had frozen over a letter on blue notepaper and he sat like a statue till he read it through. At length he raised his head; his face was expression-less. 'James, this is just about the most vitriolic letter I have ever read. It's from Cranford. He's finished with us for good and all and js considering taking legal action against us.'

'What have we done this time?' I asked.

'He accuses us of grossly insulting him and endangering the health of his boar. He says we sent him a treacle tin full of cow shit with instructions to rub it on the boar's back three times daily.'

Tristan, who had been sitting with his eyes half closed, be-came fully awake. He rose unhurriedly and began to make his way towards the door. His hand was on the knob when his brother's voice thundered out.

'Tristan! Come back here! Sit down – I think we have something to talk about.'

Tristan looked up resolutely, waiting for the storm to break, but Siegfried was unexpectedly calm. His voice was gentle.

'So you've done it again. When will I ever learn that I can't trust you to carry out the simplest task. It wasn't much to ask, was it? Two little parcels to post – hardly a tough assignment. But you managed to botch it. You got the labels wrong, didn't you?'

Tristan wriggled in his chair. 'I'm sorry, I can't think how . . .'

Siegfried held up his hand. 'Oh, don't worry. Your usual luck has come to your aid. With anybody else this bloomer would be catastrophic but with Cranford – it's like divine providence.' He paused for a moment and a dreamy expression crept into his eyes. 'The label said to work it well in with the fingers, I seem to recall. And Mr Cranford says he opened the package at the breakfast table . . . Yes, Tristan, I think you have found the way. This, I do believe, has done it.'

I said, 'But how about the legal action?'

'Oh, I think we can forget about that. Mr Cranford has a great sense of his own dignity. Just think how it would sound in court.' He crumpled the letter and dropped it into the waste paper basket. 'Well, let's get on with some work.'

He led the way out and stopped abruptly in the passage. He turned to face us. 'There's another thing, of course. I wonder how the lab is making out, testing that ointment for Johne's disease?'

CHAPTER THIRTY

I was really worried about Tricki this time. I had pulled up my car when I saw him in the street with his mistress and I was shocked at his appearance. He had become hugely fat, like a bloated sausage with a leg at each corner. His eyes, bloodshot and rheumy, stared straight ahead and his tongue lolled from his jaws.

Mrs Pumphrey hastened to explain. 'He was so listless, Mr Herriot. He seemed to have no energy. I thought he must be suffering from malnutrition, so I have been giving him some little extras between meals to build him up. Some calf's foot jelly and malt and cod liver oil and a bowl of Horlick's at night to make him sleep – nothing much really.'

'And did you cut down on the sweet things as I told you?'

'Oh, I did for a bit, but he seemed to be so weak. I had to relent. He does love cream cakes and chocolates so. I can't bear to refuse him.'

I looked down again at the little dog. That was the trouble. Tricki's only fault was greed. He had never been known to refuse food; he would tackle a meal at any hour of the day or night. And I wondered about all the things Mrs Pumphrey hadn't mentioned; the pâté on thin biscuits, the fudge, the rich trifles – Tricki loved them all.

'Are you giving him plenty of exercise?'

'Well, he has his little walks with me as you can see, but Hodgkin has been down with lumbago, so there has been no ring-throwing lately.'

I tried to sound severe. 'Now I really mean this. If you don't cut his food right down and give him more exercise he is going to be really ill. You must harden your heart and keep him on a very strict diet.'

Mrs Pumphrey wrung her hands. 'Oh I will, Mr Herriot. I'm sure you are right, but it is so difficult, so very difficult.' She set off, head down, along the road, as if determined to put the new regime into practice immediately.

I watched their progress with growing concern. Tricki was tottering along in his little tweed coat; he had a whole wardrobe of these coats – warm tweed or tartan ones for the cold weather and macintoshes for the wet days. He struggled on, drooping in his harness. I thought it wouldn't be long before I heard from Mrs Pumphrey.

The expected call came within a few days. Mrs Pumphrey was distraught. Tricki would eat nothing. Refused even his favourite dishes; and besides, he had bouts of vomiting. He spent all his time lying on a rug, panting. Didn't go for walks, didn't want to do anything.

I had made my plans in advance. The only way was to get Tricki out of the house for a period. I suggested that he be hospitalized for about a fortnight to be kept under observation.

The poor lady almost swooned. She had never been separated from her darling before; she was sure he would pine and die if he did not see her every day.

But I took a firm line. Tricki was very ill and this was the only way to save him; in fact, I thought it best to take him without delay and, followed by Mrs Pumphrey's wailings, I marched out to the car carrying the little dog wrapped in a blanket.

The entire staff was roused and maids rushed in and out bringing his day bed, his night bed, favourite cushions, toys and rubber rings, breakfast bowl, lunch bowl, supper bowl. Realizing that my car would never hold all the stuff, I started to drive away. As I moved off, Mrs Pumphrey, with a despairing cry, threw an armful of the little coats through the window. I looked in the mirror before I turned the corner of the drive; everybody was in tears.

Out on the road, I glanced down at the pathetic little animal gasping on the seat by my side. I patted the head and Tricki made a brave effort to wag his tail. 'Poor old lad,' I said, 'You haven't a kick in you but I think I know a cure for you.'

At the surgery, the household dogs surged round me. Tricki looked down at the noisy pack with dull eyes and, when put down, lay motionless on the carpet. The other dogs, after sniffing round him for a few seconds, decided he was an uninteresting object and ignored him.

I made up a bed for him in a warm loose box next to the one where the other dogs slept. For two days I kept an eye on him, giving him no food but plenty of water. At the end of the second day he started to show some interest in his surroundings and on the third he began to whimper when he heard the dogs in the yard.

When I opened the door, Tricki trotted out and was immediately engulfed by Joe the greyhound and his friends. After rolling him over and thoroughly inspecting him, the dogs moved off down the garden. Tricki followed them, rolling slightly with his surplus fat but obviously intrigued.

Later that day, I was present at feeding time. I watched while Tristan slopped the food into the bowls. There was the usual headlong rush followed by the sounds of high-speed eating; every dog knew that if he fell behind the others he was liable to have some competition for the last part of his meal.

When they had finished, Tricki took a walk round the shining bowls, licking casually inside one or two of them. Next day, an extra bowl was put out for him and I was pleased to see him jostling his way towards it.

From then on, his progress was rapid. He had no medicinal treatment of any kind but all day he ran about with the dogs, joining in their friendly scrimmages. He discovered the joys of being bowled over, trampled on and squashed every few minutes. He became an accepted member of the gang, an unlikely, silky little object among the shaggy crew, fighting like a tiger for his share at meal times and hunting rats in the old hen house at night. He had never had such a time in his life.

All the while, Mrs Pumphrey hovered anxiously in the background, ringing a dozen times a day for the latest bulletins. I dodged the questions about whether his cushions were being turned regularly or his correct coat worn according to the weather; but I was able to tell her that the little fellow was out of danger and convalescing rapidly.

The word 'convalescing' seemed to do something to Mrs Pumphrey. She started to bring round fresh eggs, two dozen at a time, to build up Tricki's strength. For a happy period there were two eggs each for breakfast, but when the bottles of sherry began to arrive, the real possibilities of the situation began to dawn on the household.

It was the same delicious vintage that I knew so well and it was to enrich Tricki's blood. Lunch became a ceremonial occasion with two glasses before and several during the meal. Siegfried and Tristan took turns at proposing Tricki's health and the standard of speechmaking improved daily. As the sponsor, I was always called upon to reply.

We could hardly believe it when the brandy came. Two bottles of Cordon Bleu, intended to put a final edge on Tricki's constitution. Siegfried dug out some balloon glasses belonging to his mother. I had never seen them before, but for a few nights they saw constant service as the fine spirit was rolled around, inhaled and reverently drunk.

They were days of deep content, starting well with the extra egg in the morning, bolstered up and sustained by the midday sherry and finishing luxuriously round the fire with the brandy.

It was a temptation to keep Tricki on as a permanent guest, but I knew Mrs Pumphrey was suffering and after a fortnight, felt compelled to phone and tell her that the little dog had recovered and was awaiting collection.

Within minutes, about thirty feet of gleaming black metal drew up outside the surgery. The chauffeur opened the door and I could just make out the figure of Mrs Pumphrey almost lost in the interior. Her hands were tightly clasped in front of her; her lips trembled. 'Oh, Mr Herriot, do tell me the truth. Is he really better?'

'Yes, he's fine. There's no need for you to get out of the car – I'll go and fetch him.'

I walked through the house into the garden. A mass of dogs was hurtling round and round the lawn and in their midst, ears flapping, tail waving, was the little golden figure of Tricki. In two weeks he had been transformed into a lithe, hard-muscled animal; he was keeping up well with the pack, stretching out in great bounds, his chest almost brushing the ground.

I carried him back along the passage to the front of the house. The chauffeur was still holding the car door open and when Tricki saw his mistress he took off from my arms in a tremendous leap and sailed into Mrs Pumphrey's lap. She gave a startled 'Ooh!' and then had to defend herself as he swarmed over her, licking her face and barking.

During the excitement, I helped the chauffeur to bring out the beds, toys, cushions, coats and bowls, none of which had been used. As the car moved away, Mrs Pumphrey leaned out of the window. Tears shone in her eyes. Her lips trembled.

'Oh, Mr Herriot,' she cried. 'How can I ever thank you? This is a triumph of surgery!'

CHAPTER THIRTY-ONE

I came suddenly and violently awake, my heart thudding and pounding in time with the insistent summons of the telephone. These bedside phones were undoubtedly an improvement on the old system when you had to gallop downstairs and stand shivering with your bare feet on the tiles of the passage; but this explosion a few inches from your ear in the small hours when the body was weak and the resistance low was shattering. I felt sure it couldn't be good for me.

The voice at the other end was offensively cheerful. 'I have a mare on foaling. She doesn't seem to be getting on wi' t'job. Reckon foal must be laid wrong – can you come and give me a hand?'

My stomach contracted to a tight ball. This was just a little bit too much; once out of bed in the middle of the night was bad enough, but twice was unfair, in fact it was sheer cruelty. I had had a hard day and had been glad to crawl between the sheets at midnight. I had been hauled out at one o'clock to a damned awkward calving and hadn't got back till nearly three. What was the time now? Three fifteen. Good God, I had only had a few minutes sleep. And a foaling! Twice as difficult as a calving as a rule. What a life! What a bloody awful life!

I muttered into the receiver, 'Right, Mr Dixon, I'll come straight away' and shuffled across the room, yawning and stretching, feeling the ache in my shoulders and arms. I looked down at the pile of clothing in the chair; I had taken them off, put them on again, taken them off already tonight and something in me rebelled at the thought of putting them on yet again. With a weary grunt I took my macintosh from the back of the door and donned it over my pyjamas, went downstairs to where my Wellingtons stood outside the dispensary door and stuck my feet into them. It was a warm night, what was the point of getting dressed up; I'd only have to strip off again at the farm.

I opened the back door and trailed slowly down the long garden, my tired mind only faintly aware of the fragrance that came from the darkness. I reached the yard at the bottom, opened the double doors into the lane and got the car out of the garage. In the silent town the buildings glowed whitely as the headlights swept across the shuttered shop fronts, the tight-drawn curtains. Everybody was asleep. Everybody except me, James Herriot, creeping sore and exhausted towards another spell of hard labour. Why the hell had I ever decided to become a country vet? I must have been crazy to pick a job where you worked seven days a week and through the night as well. Sometimes I felt as though the practice was a malignant, living entity; testing me, trying me out; putting the pressure on more and more to see just when at what point I would drop down dead.

It was a completely unconscious reaction which hoisted me from my bath of self pity and left me dripping on the brink, regarding the immediate future with a return of some of my natural optimism. For one thing, Dixon's place was down at the foot of the Dale just off the main road and they had that unusual luxury, electric light in the buildings. And I couldn't be all that tired; not at the age of twenty-four with all my faculties unimpaired. I'd take a bit of killing yet.

I smiled to myself and relapsed into the state of half suspended animation which was normal to me at these times; a sleepy blanketing of all the senses except those required for the job in hand. Many times over the past months I had got out of bed, driven far into the country, done my job efficiently and returned to bed without ever having been fully awake.

I was right about Dixon's. The graceful Clydesdale mare was in a well-lit loose box and I laid out my ropes and instruments with a feeling of deep thankfulness. As I tipped antiseptic into the steaming bucket I watched the mare straining and paddling her limbs. The effort produced nothing; there were no feet protruding from the vulva. There was almost certainly a malpresentation.

Still thinking hard, I removed my macintosh and was jerked out of my reverie by a shout of laughter from the farmer. 'God 'elp us, what's this, the Fol-de-rols?'

I looked down at my pyjamas which were pale blue with an arresting broad stripe. 'This, Mr Dixon,' I replied with dignity, 'is my night attire. I didn't bother to dress.'

'Oh, I see now.' The farmer's eyes glinted impishly. 'I'm sorry, but I thought I'd got the wrong chap for a second. I saw a feller just like you at Blackpool last year – same suit exactly, but he 'ad a stripy top hat too and a stick. Did a champion little dance.'

'Can't oblige you, I'm afraid,' I said with a wan smile. 'I'm just not in the mood right now.'

I stripped off, noting with interest the deep red grooves caused by the calf's teeth a couple of hours ago. Those teeth had been like razors, peeling off neat little rolls of skin every time I pushed my arm past them.

The mare trembled as I felt my way inside her. Nothing, nothing, then just a tail and the pelvic bones and the body and hind legs disappearing away beyond my reach. Breech presentation; easy in the cow for a man who knew his job but tricky in the mare because of the tremendous length of the foal's legs.

It took me a sweating, panting half hour with ropes and a blunt hook on the end of a flexible cane to bring the first leg round. The second leg came more easily and the mare seemed to know there was no obstruction now. She gave a great heave and the foal shot out onto the straw with myself, arms around its body, sprawling on top of it. To my delight I felt the small form jerking convulsively; I had felt no movement while I was working and had decided that it was dead, but the foal was very much alive, shaking its head and snorting out the placental fluid it had inhaled during its delayed entry.

When I had finished towelling myself I turned to see the farmer with an abnormally straight face, holding out my colourful jacket like a valet. 'Allow me, sir,' he said gravely.

'OK, OK,' I laughed, 'I'll get properly dressed next time.' As I was putting my things in the car boot the farmer carelessly threw a parcel on to the back seat.

'Bit o' butter for you,' he muttered. When I started the engine he bent level with the window. 'I think a bit about that mare and I've been badly wanting a foal out of her. Thank ye lad, thank ye very much.'

He waved as I moved away and I heard his parting cry. 'You did all right for a Kentucky Minstrel!'

I leaned back in my seat and peered through heavy lids at the empty road unwinding in the pale morning light. The sun had come up – a dark crimson ball hanging low over the misted fields. I felt utterly content, warm with the memory of the foal trying to struggle on to its knees, its absurdly long legs still out of control. Grand that the little beggar had been alive after all – there was something desolate about delivering a lifeless creature.

The Dixon farm was in the low country where the Dale widened out and gave on to the great plain of York. I had to cross a loop of the busy road which connected the West Riding with the industrial North East. A thin tendril of smoke rose from the chimney of the all night transport café which stood there and as I slowed down to take the corner a faint but piercing smell of cooking found its way into the car; the merest breath but rich in the imagery of fried sausages and beans and tomatoes and chips.

God, I was starving. I looked at my watch; five fifteen, I wouldn't be eating for a long time yet. I turned in among the lorries on the broad strip of tarmac.

Hastening towards the still lighted building I decided that I wouldn't be greedy. Nothing spectacular, just a nice sandwich. I had been here a few times before and the sandwiches were very good; and I deserved some nourishment after my hard night.

I stepped into the warm interior where groups of lorry drivers sat behind mounded plates, but as I crossed the floor the busy clatter died and was replaced by a tense silence. A fat man in a leather jacket sat transfixed, a loaded fork halfway to his mouth, while his neighbour, gripping a huge mug of tea in an oily hand stared with bulging eyes at my ensemble.

It occurred to me then that bright red striped pyjamas and Wellingtons might seem a little unusual in those surroundings and I hastily buttoned my macintosh which had been billowing behind me. Even closed, it was on the short side and at least a foot of pyjama leg showed above my boots.

Resolutely I strode over to the counter. An expressionless blonde bulging out of a dirty white overall on the breast pocket of which was inscribed 'Dora' regarded me blankly.

'A ham sandwich and a cup of Bovril, please,' I said huskily. As the blonde put a teaspoonful of Bovril into a cup and filled it with a hissing jet of hot water I was uncomfortably aware of the silence behind me and of the battery of eyes focused on my legs. On my right I could just see the leather jacketed man. He filled his mouth and chewed reflectively for a few moments.

'Takes all kinds, don't it Ernest,' he said in a judicial tone.

'Does indeed, Kenneth, does indeed,' replied his companion.

'Would you say, Ernest, that this is what the Yorkshire country gentleman is wearing this spring?'

'Could be, Kenneth, could be.'

Listening to the titters from the rear, I concluded that these two were the accepted café wags. Best to eat up quickly and get out. Dora pushed the thickly meated sandwich across the counter and spoke with all the animation of a sleep walker. 'That'll be a shillin'.'

I slipped my hand inside my coat and encountered the pocketless flannelette beneath. God almighty, my money was in my trousers back in Darrowby! A wave of sickly horror flooded me as I began a frantic, meaningless search through my macintosh.

I looked wildly at the blonde and saw her slip the sandwich under the counter. 'Look, I've come out without any money. I've been in here before – do you know who I am?'

Dora gave a single bored shake of her head.

'Well, never mind,' I babbled, 'I'll pop in with the money next time I'm passing.'

Dora's expression did not alter but she raised one eyebrow fractionally; she made no effort to retrieve the sandwich from its hiding place.

Escape was the only thing in my mind now. Desperately I sipped at the scalding fluid.

Kenneth pushed back his plate and began to pick his teeth with a match. 'Ernest,' he said as though coming to a weighty conclusion. 'It's my opinion that this 'ere gentleman is eccentric.'

'Eccentric?' Ernest sniggered into his tea. 'Bloody daft, more like.'

'Ah, but not so daft, Ernest. Not daft enough to pay for 'is grub.'

'You 'ave a point there, Kenneth, a definite point.'

'You bet I have. He's enjoying a nice cup of Bovril on the house and if 'e hadn't mistimed his fumble he'd be at the sandwich too. Dora moved a bit sharpish for 'im there – another five seconds and he'd have had 'is choppers in the ham.'

'True, true,' muttered Ernest, seemingly content with his role of straight man.

Kenneth put away his match, sucked his teeth noisily and leaned back. 'There's another possibility we 'aven't considered. He could be on the run.'

'Escaped convict, you mean, Kenneth.'

'I do, Ernest, I do indeed.'

'But them fellers allus have arrows on their uniforms.'

'Ah, some of 'em do. But I 'eard somewhere that some of the prisons is going in for stripes now.'

I had had enough. Tipping the last searing drops of Bovril down my throat I made headlong for the door. As I stepped out into the early sunshine Kenneth's final pronouncement reached me.

'Prob'ly got away from a working party. Look at them Wellingtons ...'

POSTSCRIPT

I remember it was an afternoon when the sun blazed. I filled my car with Siegfried's dogs and drove to where an old mine track climbed green and inviting on the side of a steep gill. We walked a mile or two on the smooth turf then turned off and headed straight up the hillside through the hot bracken scent and the hum of flies to the very top where the wind was sweet and welcome and you could see nearly all of the Dale laid out there beneath; nearly all of it from the head where the great bare hills stood on the edge of the wild right down to the rich plain, chequered and hazy, at the foot.

I was sitting in the heather with the dogs in an expectant ring when the Dales smell came up on the breeze, the fragrance which the wind stole from the miles of warm grass and the shy flowers of the moorland. It had met me when I first stepped off the bus at Darrowby a year ago. And I realized that I had worked my way through the full cycle: I had travelled that magical first time round.

And it had all happened down there. Many of the farms in the practice were visible from where I sat; splashes of grey stone with their livestock, motionless dots from this distance, scattered in the fields around them. They were unrecognizable as the battle grounds of the past year, the scenes of my first struggles where everything had happened from heady success to abject failure.

There were people down there who thought I was a pretty fair vet, some who regarded me as an amiable idiot, a few who were convinced I was a genius and one or two who would set their dogs on me if I put a foot inside their gates.

All this in a year. What would be the position in thirty years? Well, as it turned out, very much the same.

And what of the animals around whom the whole little

drama revolves? It is a pity they cannot talk because it would be charming to have their views. There are a few things I would like to know. What do they think of their widely varying lives? What do they think of us? And do they manage to get a laugh out of it all?